I0411253

Table of Contents

Forget avocado toast and lattes – it's time to re-define #financiallyindependent. This ain't your grandma's "get a job, climb the ladder" guide. We're talking side hustles so hot, they may explode your bank accounts. This little book isn't just about making money, it's about owning your future, crafting a life that doesn't bend to office hours or fluorescent lights.

Imagine waking up to the dopamine rush of a sale notification on your phone – not the stale ding of your alarm clock. Picture your passion birthing not just epic memes, but a thriving online empire. Feel the electric surge of launching your own platform, where you're the CEO, the creator, the captain of your own financial destiny. That's the Gen Z Money manifesto, baby.

This ain't a one-size-fits-all roadmap, though. You're a kaleidoscope of skills, a walking algorithm of potential. So we're serving up a buffet of options, a smorgasbord of side hustles to ignite your unique spark. Want to turn your graphic design skills into walking billboards with Print-on-Demand? Do it. Got a blog overflowing with your witty takes on #everything? Monetize that magic, word warrior. We'll show you how to transform your digital footprint into a cash-generating machine.

But hold up, this ain't just about selling stuff. We're talking influence, yo. Imagine commanding an audience that hangs on your every post, your videos, and your podcasts. We'll show you how to build that tribe, how to become a social media oracle, a YouTube star, a voice that resonates deeper than your latest Spotify playlist.

And yeah, we're dipping our toes in the crypto pool too, because Gen Z doesn't shy away from the cutting edge. We'll demystify the lingo, break down the blockchain, and show you how to navigate the future of finance with confidence.

But it ain't all hustle and hype, fam. We're not here to leave you burnt out with a side of anxiety. Mastering productivity is part of the package. We'll show you how to hack your time, optimize your workflow, and conquer your goals without sacrificing your sanity.

It's a potential gateway to your financial liberation, a launchpad to a life that's anything but ordinary. We're talking freedom, flexibility, and enough Benjamins to finally ditch the ramen diet. Let's rewrite the rules of the game, together. This is more than a book, it's a movement. It's Gen Z Money, and the revolution starts now.

Chapter I

Print On Demand (POD)

Unleashing Creativity and Profits with a Print-On-Demand Empire

In the vast landscape of entrepreneurial possibilities, one avenue has captured the hearts and minds of the tech-savvy and creative Gen Z demographic - the Print-on-Demand (POD) business. Imagine turning your passion for design and innovation into a lucrative venture without the hassle of inventory management. It's not just a dream; it's the Print-on-Demand revolution, tailor-made for the digitally fluent generation.

Understanding the Print-on-Demand Model

Before we dive into the exciting world of Print-on-Demand, let's demystify the model. At its core, POD is a business strategy that allows entrepreneurs to create and sell custom-designed products without maintaining a physical inventory. From T-shirts and mugs to phone cases and wall art, the possibilities are as endless as your imagination.

Why Gen Z?

Gen Z, born between the mid-1990s and early 2010s, is known for its entrepreneurial spirit, digital prowess, and relentless pursuit of individualism. This generation is not just consumers; they are creators, seeking avenues to express their unique identities. The Print-on-Demand business aligns perfectly with these traits, offering a platform for self-expression and the potential for substantial profits.

The Blueprint: Setting Up Your Print-on-Demand Business

Niche Discovery

The first step in your POD journey is identifying your niche. What makes you tick? Is it eco-friendly fashion, quirky memes, or empowering slogans? Your niche will be the foundation of your brand, connecting you with a like-minded audience.

According to a study by Shopify, successful POD businesses often thrive by catering to specific niches, as it allows for targeted marketing and a dedicated customer base.

Market Research

Understanding your target audience is paramount. Utilize social media, surveys, and online forums to gather insights into their preferences and pain points. Platforms like Instagram and TikTok are goldmines for Gen Z market research.

A report from Statista reveals that 81% of Gen Z use Instagram regularly, making it a prime platform for brand discovery and engagement.

Designing Your Products

Let your creativity run wild! Invest time in creating unique, eye-catching designs that resonate with your chosen niche. Remember, authenticity is key for Gen Z consumers.

A survey by Pew Research Center highlights that 81% of Gen Z values authenticity in the brands they support.

Platform Selection

Choosing the right platform is crucial. Shopify, Printful, and Printify are popular choices for setting up a Print-on-Demand store. They offer user-friendly interfaces and integrate seamlessly with various e-commerce platforms.

According to a survey by Oberlo, 27% of entrepreneurs prefer Shopify for its ease of use and versatility.

Marketing Magic

Leverage social media to build brand awareness. Platforms like Instagram and TikTok are ideal for visually appealing products. Engage in influencer collaborations and user-generated content campaigns to create buzz around your brand.

The GlobalWebIndex Social Media Flagship Report states that 62% of Gen Z and Millennials discover new brands through social media.

Motivating Facts: Fuel for Your Entrepreneurial Spirit

1. Lucrative Market Potential

The global Print-on-Demand market is projected to reach $10.4 billion by 2025, according to a report by Grand View Research. This represents a compound annual growth rate (CAGR) of 9.9% from 2018 to 2025.

2. Minimal Risk, Maximum Reward

POD eliminates the need for upfront investment in inventory. You only produce items when customers place orders, significantly reducing the financial risks associated with traditional retail models.

3. Empowering Small Businesses

Print-on-demand levels the playing field, empowering small businesses and independent artists to compete with established brands. With minimal overhead costs, the barrier to entry is lower than ever.

Your Journey Begins

Embarking on a Print-on-Demand venture is not just a business move; it's a journey of self-discovery and empowerment. The convergence of creative expression, digital entrepreneurship, and minimal risk makes POD an ideal choice for the dynamic and ambitious Gen Z demographic. Armed with the right tools, a unique vision, and a sprinkle of passion, your Print-on-Demand empire awaits. Seize the opportunity, and let your creativity leave an indelible mark on the world.

How to Start a Print-on-Demand Business

Starting a print-on-demand business can be broken down into several key steps:

Choose a niche with high-profit products: Select a niche that has a demand for custom products and offers high-profit margins. Research popular niches and analyze their potential for profitability

Create engaging artwork: Design unique and appealing products that resonate with your target audience. You can use design tools, and software, or even hire a professional designer to help you create eye-catching designs

Set up your online store: Choose an e-commerce platform, such as Shopify, and create a visually appealing and user-friendly online store that showcases your products

Choose a fulfillment partner: Select a reliable print-on-demand service (Printful, Printify, Amazon and others) that aligns with your niche and product offerings. They will handle the manufacturing and shipping process when an order is placed

Strategize shipping: Ensure your fulfillment partner has multiple factories in various countries to provide faster shipping options and better shipping costs

Use attractive mockups: Showcase your products in appealing mockups to make them more visually appealing to potential customers

Develop a marketing plan: Promote your products through social media, content marketing, and other online channels. Consider using influencer marketing or offering promotions to attract customers

Monitor and optimize: Continuously analyze your sales data, customer feedback, and market trends to identify areas for improvement and adjust your strategy accordingly.

Navigating Challenges and Scaling Heights - Building Print-on-Demand Empire

As you embark on your Print-on-Demand journey, it's crucial to understand that challenges are part and parcel of the entrepreneurial experience. In this chapter, we'll explore common hurdles faced by POD businesses and equip you with strategies to overcome them, ensuring your venture not only survives but thrives.

1. Quality Control

Ensuring the quality of your products is paramount. POD businesses rely on third-party printing services, making it essential to choose partners with a reputation for delivering high-quality items. Regularly order samples to assess the final product's quality and make adjustments as needed.

Strategies:

- Research and choose reliable printing partners with positive reviews.

- Request and thoroughly evaluate product samples before adding new items to your store.

2. Shipping Woes

Shipping times and costs can be a headache for both you and your customers. Delays and unexpected fees can lead to dissatisfaction. Optimize your shipping strategy by working with reliable carriers and clearly communicating expected delivery times.

Strategies:

- Clearly communicate shipping policies on your website.

- Offer transparent tracking options to keep customers informed.

- Consider partnering with fulfillment services to expedite shipping.

3. Design Theft and Copyright Issues

The digital world comes with its share of challenges, including the risk of design theft and copyright infringement. Protect your intellectual property by watermarking designs and understanding copyright laws.

Strategies:

- Research and stay informed about copyright laws.

- Use watermarks on product images to deter theft.

- Consider registering trademarks for your brand and designs.

4. Market Saturation

As the Print-on-Demand industry continues to flourish, competition is fierce. Standing out amidst a sea of products requires constant innovation, unique designs, and strategic marketing.

Strategies:

- Regularly refresh your product offerings with new designs.

- Leverage data analytics to identify and capitalize on emerging trends.

- Invest in targeted marketing to reach your niche audience effectively.

Data and Motivating Insights

1. Consumer Loyalty and Brand Consistency

According to a survey by McKinsey, 64% of consumers around the world cite shared values as the primary reason for developing a strong brand relationship. Consistency in your brand messaging, designs, and customer experience builds trust and loyalty among your audience.

2. Sustainable Practices Matter

Gen Z is environmentally conscious, with 72% stating that they are willing to pay more for sustainable products, as reported by Nielsen. Embrace eco-friendly practices in your Print-on-Demand business, from using organic materials to reducing packaging waste.

3. The Power of Customer Reviews

Positive reviews hold immense sway over potential customers. A study by BrightLocal reveals that 86% of consumers read reviews for local businesses, emphasizing the importance of maintaining high-quality products and exceptional customer service.

Scaling Your Print-on-Demand Business

1. Diversify Product Offerings

Expand your product range to cater to different tastes within your niche. Consider adding complementary items or seasonal collections to keep customers engaged and boost revenue.

2. Harness Data for Growth

Leverage analytics tools to gather insights into customer behavior, popular products, and emerging trends. Use this data to refine your marketing strategies, optimize your product lineup, and identify areas for improvement.

3. Collaborate and Network

Forge partnerships with influencers, fellow entrepreneurs, and complementary brands to expand your reach. Collaborative efforts can introduce your brand to new audiences and foster a sense of community around your products.

4. Invest in Marketing

Allocate resources to strategic marketing efforts, including social media advertising, email campaigns, and influencer partnerships. Consistent and targeted marketing is key to maintaining brand visibility and attracting new customers.

Crafting a Resilient Future

Navigating the challenges of the Print-on-Demand landscape requires resilience, adaptability, and a keen eye for innovation. By addressing common hurdles head-on and implementing strategic solutions, your Print-on-Demand empire can not only weather the storms but also reach new heights of success. Embrace the journey, learn from every experience, and let each challenge sculpt a more resilient and thriving business. Your Print-on-Demand empire is not just a business; it's a legacy in the making.

Adapting to Trends and Future-Proofing Your Print-on-Demand Empire

Embracing the Ever-Evolving Landscape

As your Print-on-Demand (POD) business matures, it becomes essential to not only meet current consumer demands but also to anticipate and adapt to future trends. In this chapter, we'll explore the dynamic nature of the POD industry, offering insights on staying ahead of the curve and future-proofing your empire.

The Dynamic Nature of Print-on-Demand

1. Embracing Tech Innovations

The rapid pace of technological advancements presents both challenges and opportunities. Stay abreast of new printing technologies, design tools, and e-commerce platforms. Embrace innovations that enhance the customer experience and streamline your operations.

Strategies:

- Explore augmented reality (AR) for virtual product try-ons.

- Incorporate AI tools for personalized shopping recommendations.

- Experiment with eco-friendly printing methods and materials.

2. Sustainability as a Driving Force

Environmental consciousness is no longer a trend but a core value for consumers, particularly among Gen Z. Adopting sustainable practices not only aligns with ethical standards but also attracts a growing segment of environmentally conscious buyers.

Strategies:

- Source eco-friendly materials and packaging.

- Communicate your commitment to sustainability in marketing materials.

- Consider implementing carbon-neutral shipping options.

Data and Motivating Insights

1. Mobile-First Shopping

With 98% of Gen Z owning a smartphone, according to a study by Pew Research Center, optimizing your online store for mobile devices is non-negotiable. Ensure a seamless mobile shopping experience to capture the attention of this tech-savvy demographic.

2. Social Commerce

The intersection of social media and e-commerce is a burgeoning trend. Utilize features like Instagram Shops and Facebook Marketplace to directly sell products on popular social platforms. The ease of discovery and seamless shopping experience can significantly boost your sales.

3. Customization and Personalization

Consumers, especially Gen Z, crave unique, personalized experiences. Implement customization options on your products, allowing customers to add their touch to designs. This fosters a sense of ownership and connection with your brand.

Adapting to Future Trends

1. Cryptocurrency Adoption

The rise of cryptocurrencies is reshaping the online business landscape. Consider accepting cryptocurrencies as a form of payment, tapping into a tech-forward demographic, and positioning your business at the forefront of financial innovation.

2. Virtual and Augmented Reality Experiences

Integrate virtual and augmented reality technologies to provide immersive shopping experiences. This can include virtual try-ons, AR-enhanced product previews, and interactive elements that engage customers on a new level.

3. Community Building and User-Generated Content

Build a community around your brand by encouraging user-generated content. This not only fosters a sense of belonging but also serves as authentic marketing. Consider creating forums, hosting contests, and featuring customer stories on your platform.

Crafting a Future-Ready Legacy

Adapting to the ever-evolving landscape of the Print-on-Demand industry requires a combination of foresight, agility, and a commitment to innovation. As you integrate new technologies, embrace sustainability, and anticipate consumer trends, you position your Print-on-Demand empire as not just a business but a dynamic force shaping the future of retail. Seize the opportunities presented by emerging trends, stay connected with your audience, and let your Print-on-Demand legacy evolve into a resilient and visionary brand. The future is yours to craft.

Chapter II

Launching and Monetizing a Blog

Pour Your Heart into Writing Content That Brings You Benjamin

Welcome to the world of blogging, where your passion and creativity can be transformed into a profitable business. In this chapter, we will explore the exciting journey of starting and monetizing a blog, tailored to the Gen Z demographic. From creating engaging content to various monetization strategies, this guide will provide you with the essential knowledge and tools to turn your blog into a successful and sustainable business.

In the ever-evolving landscape of digital entrepreneurship, blogging stands out as a gateway for Gen Z individuals to carve their niche and unleash their creativity. With the power of the internet at their fingertips, this demographic is uniquely positioned to leverage their skills and perspectives to create engaging and profitable blogs. This chapter will guide you through the process of starting and monetizing a blog, providing insights, data, and motivating facts to inspire and empower the next generation of online content creators.

To set up your blog. Choose a suitable platform and domain, and customize it to reflect your unique voice and brand. Building a blog gives you control over your business and access to your audience in a way social media can't, offering leverage, scale, and sustainability.

Unleashing Your Passion

The first step in starting a successful blog is identifying your passion and niche. Gen Z is known for its diverse interests, making it crucial to choose a topic that not only excites you but also resonates with your target audience. Whether it's sustainability, fashion, tech, or social justice, your passion will be the driving force behind your blog's success.

According to a study by GlobalWebIndex, 42% of Gen Z individuals are interested in sustainable and eco-friendly living. Pew Research Center reports that Gen Z is more racially and ethnically diverse than previous generations, highlighting the importance of addressing diverse perspectives in your content.

Building a Unique Brand

In a crowded online space, a strong and unique brand is essential for standing out. Consider your blog as a personal brand and invest time in designing a visually appealing website, creating a memorable logo, and defining your tone of voice. Building a cohesive brand identity will make your blog easily recognizable and memorable for your audience.

Wyzowl's State of Video Marketing report reveals that 81% of businesses believe that video marketing has helped increase their brand awareness. According to Adobe, consistent branding across all channels can increase revenue by up to 23%.

Content is King

Quality content is the backbone of a successful blog. Create engaging, informative, and shareable content to capture and retain your audience's attention. Utilize multimedia elements such as images, videos, and infographics to enhance the overall user experience.

HubSpot's Content Trends report indicates that 70% of marketers actively invest in content marketing. Social Media Today reports that posts with images receive 2.3 times more engagement on social media platforms.

Monetizing Your Blog

Once you've established your blog and built a dedicated audience, it's time to explore monetization strategies. Gen Z entrepreneurs can tap into various revenue streams, such as sponsored content, affiliate marketing, digital products, and more.

A survey by Mediakix found that 89% of marketers find influencer marketing effective for achieving their objectives. According to the Interactive Advertising Bureau (IAB), affiliate marketing spending is expected to reach $8.2 billion by 2022.

Monetization is a marathon, not a sprint. It's important to think of it as a long-term commitment. There are various ways to monetize your blog, including advertising, affiliate marketing, digital products, services, membership, and crowdfunding

It's essential to choose a business model that works for you and aligns with your content and audience

Motivating Facts

While the journey of monetizing a blog requires time and effort, the potential rewards are significant. With the right strategy and dedication, it's possible to turn a blog into a profitable business. Many successful bloggers have capitalized on their content and turned it into a viable business, generating substantial income and enjoying the freedom to pursue what they love

Starting and monetizing a blog is a rewarding and potentially lucrative endeavor. By following the steps outlined in this guide and staying committed to creating valuable content and implementing effective monetization strategies, you can turn your blog into a successful and sustainable business.

For further details and in-depth insights, the provided sources offer valuable information and guidance on various aspects of starting and monetizing a blog.

Staying Authentic

Gen Z values authenticity, and maintaining genuine connections with your audience is crucial for long-term success. Avoid compromising your values for quick profits and prioritize building trust with your audience. Authenticity not only enhances your brand reputation but also fosters a loyal and engaged community.

A study by Stackla found that 90% of consumers believe authenticity is important when deciding which brands to support. Nielsen's Global Trust in Advertising report states that 83% of consumers trust recommendations from people they know.

Create Engaging Contents

To create engaging content for a blog, it's important to consider the following key strategies:

Understand Your Audience: Choose topics that resonate with your audience and address their interests and needs.

Craft Compelling Headlines: Create attention-grabbing headlines that entice readers to explore your content further.

Make Content Scannable: Structure your content for easy scanning by using subheadings, bullet points, and short paragraphs.

Use Visuals: Incorporate images, infographics, and videos to enhance the visual appeal of your content and engage your audience.

Encourage Interaction: Include elements such as polls, quizzes, and interactive slideshows to make your content more engaging and interactive.

Tell a Story: Use storytelling to make your content more relatable and emotionally compelling.

Maintain a Conversational Tone: Write in a friendly and informal tone to connect with your readers on a personal level.

Include Call to Action: Encourage reader engagement by including a call to action, such as asking for comments or feedback.

By implementing these strategies, you can create blog content that captivates your audience and keeps them coming back for more.

Starting and monetizing a blog as a Gen Z entrepreneur is an exciting journey filled with endless possibilities. By combining your passion with a strong brand, high-quality content, and authentic engagement, you can create a blog that not only resonates with your audience but also generates revenue. As you embark on this adventure, remember that success takes time, dedication, and a commitment to staying true to yourself and your values.

Niche Selection and Topic Ideation: Tailoring Your Blog for Success

Choosing the right niche and topics is the foundation of a successful blog. In this chapter, we'll explore strategies to help Gen Z entrepreneurs identify a niche that aligns with their passions, resonates with their target audience, and has the potential for long-term success.

Discovering Your Passion

Your journey into the blogosphere begins with introspection. Identify your passions, hobbies, and interests. Your blog is an extension of yourself, and your enthusiasm will be the driving force behind its creation. Whether it's gaming, sustainability, travel, or personal development, choose a niche that genuinely excites you.

A study by Harvard Business Review suggests that passion is a key factor in entrepreneurial success. According to Gallup, people who use their strengths at work are more engaged and productive.

Analyzing Market Trends

While passion is crucial, it's equally important to analyze market trends to ensure there's an audience for your chosen niche. Use tools like Google Trends, social media insights, and industry reports to identify rising trends and potential gaps in the market.

Google Trends can provide real-time data on the popularity of search queries, helping you identify trending topics. The Global Entrepreneurship Monitor (GEM) report highlights the importance of market research in identifying business opportunities.

Understanding Your Target Audience

A successful blog speaks directly to its target audience. Define your ideal reader by considering demographics, interests, and pain points.

Understand what your audience is searching for and tailor your content to meet their needs. A study by the Content Marketing Institute found that 63% of successful content marketers have a documented audience strategy. Nielsen Norman Group emphasizes the importance of creating user personas to guide content creation.

Evaluating Competition

Competition can be fierce in certain niches, so it's crucial to assess your potential competitors. Identify key players in your chosen niche, analyze their content, and identify areas where you can offer a unique perspective or fill gaps in the market.

Competitor analysis tools like SEMrush and Ahrefs can provide insights into your competitors' strategies and keyword rankings. The Harvard Business Review suggests that understanding competitors is essential for strategic decision-making.

Balancing Passion and Profitability

While passion is the driving force, it's essential to find a balance between what you love and what has the potential for profitability. Evaluate potential revenue streams within your chosen niche, such as affiliate marketing, sponsored content, or selling digital products.

A report by Business Insider states that 86% of women and 74% of men are more likely to trust influencers' recommendations. The Content Marketing Institute highlights the diverse monetization options available to content creators.

Choosing the right niche and topics for your blog is a crucial step in your entrepreneurial journey. By combining your passion with market analysis, understanding your audience, evaluating competition, and finding the sweet spot between passion and profitability, you'll set the stage for a blog that not only resonates with your audience but also stands the test of time. Embrace the process, stay authentic, and watch as your blog becomes a beacon in your chosen niche.

Monetizing your Blog: A Step-by-Step Guide

Turning your passion into profit is the dream for many bloggers. But where do you begin? This guide will equip you with a comprehensive plan to monetize your blog, from building a strong foundation to implementing various income streams. Remember, success takes time and effort, so be patient, consistent, and adaptable.

Assess your blog's readiness

Traffic and engagement: Do you have a consistent audience base? Can you measure their engagement through comments, shares, or newsletter signups? A minimum of 1000 monthly visitors is a good starting point.

Niche and expertise: Is your niche clearly defined? Do you offer unique insights or valuable information within your area? Strong niche focus attracts targeted readers and relevant monetization opportunities.

Content quality: Are your blog posts well-written, informative, and engaging? High-quality content keeps readers coming back and builds trust.

Choose your monetization strategy

Advertising: Display ads (banners, pop-ups) generate revenue based on impressions or clicks. Platforms like Google AdSense offer targeted ad options.

Affiliate marketing: Promote other companies' products through affiliate links. You earn a commission when readers purchase through your links. Choose relevant products your audience trusts.

Digital products: Create and sell ebooks, online courses, templates, or printables related to your niche. Offer valuable solutions to audience problems.

Premium content: Create exclusive content for paying subscribers, like in-depth guides, bonus resources, or early access to new posts.

Sponsored content: Partner with brands for sponsored posts, product reviews, or brand mentions. Ensure transparency and align with your blog's values.

Consulting/coaching: Leverage your expertise by offering freelance writing, consulting services, or coaching programs in your niche.

Donations: Allow readers to support your work through voluntary donations using platforms like PayPal.

Implement your chosen strategy

Optimize your website: Ensure your blog is user-friendly, fast-loading, and mobile-responsive. Prioritize SEO best practices for increased organic traffic.

Build an email list: Encourage readers to subscribe to your newsletter to nurture relationships and promote exclusive content.

Track your results: Analyze data from analytics tools to understand what's working and what's not. Adapt your strategy based on insights.

Promote your monetization efforts: Clearly communicate your income streams through ads, calls to action, and dedicated pages. Offer value propositions for each option.

Network with other bloggers: Collaborate with others in your niche for cross-promotion, guest blogging opportunities, and shared learning.

Be patient and adaptable

Building a successful monetized blog takes time. Experiment with different strategies, tweak your approach, and continuously improve your content and user experience. Stay updated on industry trends and adapt your monetization methods as needed.

Focus on providing value to your audience: Always prioritize reader benefit over revenue. High-quality content builds trust and encourages engagement.

Be transparent and ethical: Disclose sponsored content, affiliate relationships, and potential conflicts of interest. Build trust with your audience.

Diversify your income streams: Don't rely on one single source of revenue. Mix and match different monetization options to create a stable income flow.

Enjoy the process: Blogging should be fun and fulfilling. Celebrate your successes and learn from your setbacks.

Remember, monetization is just one aspect of successful blogging. By focusing on creating valuable content, building a loyal audience, and constantly learning and adapting, you can turn your blog into a thriving platform for both passion and profit.

Mastering Social Media and SEO for Blog Growth

In the fast-paced world of digital entrepreneurship, mastering the art of online visibility is essential for the success of your blog. In this chapter, we'll delve into leveraging social media and search engine optimization (SEO) strategies to boost your blog's reach, engage a broader audience, and drive organic traffic.

The Power of Social Media

Social media platforms have become indispensable tools for reaching and connecting with audiences. Gen Z, being digital natives, is well-versed in the dynamics of platforms like Instagram, TikTok, Twitter, and LinkedIn. Utilizing these platforms strategically can exponentially increase your blog's visibility. According to Statista, the number of global social media users is expected to reach 3.6 billion by 2025. A study by GlobalWebIndex reveals that the average daily time spent on social media is approximately 2 hours and 31 minutes.

Crafting Shareable Content

Creating content that is shareable and resonates with your target audience is a key component of social media success. Whether its eye-catching visuals, engaging captions, or thought-provoking videos, tailor your content to each platform's unique style while staying true to your brand.

Hootsuite's Social Media Trends report indicates that 64% of consumers want brands to connect with them on social media. Social Media Examiner reports that 58% of marketers consider original written content the most important form of content.

Building an SEO Strategy

Search engine optimization is the cornerstone of organic traffic growth. Understanding how search engines work and implementing SEO best practices will ensure that your blog ranks higher in search results, driving more traffic to your site.

According to Moz, the first page of Google captures 71% of search traffic clicks. Backlinko's analysis of 5 million Google search results found that the average word count of a first-page result is 1,890 words.

Keyword Research and Implementation

Effective SEO begins with comprehensive keyword research. Identify keywords and phrases relevant to your niche and integrate them seamlessly into your content. Tools like Google Keyword

Planner, SEMrush, and Ahrefs can aid in discovering high-performing keywords.

Ahrefs reports that 91% of web content gets zero organic traffic from Google due to not having any backlinks. HubSpot's State of Marketing report shows that 68% of marketers use paid advertising to discover high-performing keywords.

Engaging with Your Community

Social media and SEO efforts should not be one-sided. Actively engage with your audience by responding to comments, participating in discussions, and seeking feedback. Building a sense of community around your blog fosters loyalty and encourages organic growth through word-of-mouth.

A survey by Sprout Social found that 40% of consumers expect brands to respond within the first hour of reaching out on social media. Social Media Today reports that 71% of consumers who have a positive experience with a brand on social media are likely to recommend it to others.

In the dynamic landscape of the digital world, mastering social media and SEO is paramount for blog success. By strategically using platforms, crafting shareable content, implementing SEO best practices, and engaging with your community, you'll amplify your blog's reach and create a lasting impact on your audience. Stay adaptable, stay informed, and watch as your blog flourishes in the vast digital ecosystem.

Chapter III

Create and Sell Digital Product Online

Revolutionizing Commerce for Gen Z – Build Business at Your Desk.

Welcome to the world of selling digital products. In the digital age, the landscape of commerce has undergone a seismic shift, and at the forefront of this revolution is the dynamic world of selling digital products. For the trailblazing Generation Z, born into a world immersed in technology, this business model is not just a trend; it's a way of life. As we embark on this journey, let's delve into the exciting realm of selling digital products, exploring its roots, understanding its impact, and uncovering the secrets to success.

The transition from traditional commerce to the digital marketplace has been swift, and Gen Z has been quick to embrace this change. According to a survey by Business News Daily, 72% of Gen Z aspire to start their own business. Selling digital products provides an accessible avenue for these ambitious individuals to channel their creativity and carve out a niche in the vast digital landscape.

Understanding Digital Products

In today's digital age, digital products are items that can be owned and used on mobile gadgets. They are intangible goods or services that can be created once and sold repeatedly, offering the freedom to focus solely on improving the products. Examples of digital products include e-books, online courses, templates, software, and downloadable designs.

Popular Digital Products and Where to Sell Them

1. Digital Art and Graphics

Platforms: Etsy, Gumroad, or create a personal website.

2. eBooks and Online Courses

Platforms: Amazon Kindle Direct Publishing (KDP), Udemy, Teachable.

3. Stock Photography and Videos

Platforms: Shutterstock, Adobe Stock, or start your own stock media website.

4. Mobile Apps and Games

Platforms: Apple App Store, Google Play, or independent app marketplaces.

5. Web Templates and Themes

Platforms: ThemeForest, Creative Market, or sell directly on your website.

6. Digital Music and Sound Effects

Platforms: Bandcamp, SoundCloud, or license to filmmakers and content creators.

7. Printables and Planners:

Platforms: Etsy, Shopify, or sell through social media.

8. Virtual Services and Consultations

Platforms: Fiverr, Upwork, or create a personal consulting website.

These digital products can be sold on various platforms such as your own website, online marketplaces like Amazon, Etsy, and eBay, or specialized platforms like Udemy, Skillshare, and Teachable.

Identifying Your Niche and Target Audience

Before diving into the world of selling digital products, it's essential to identify your niche and target audience. Understanding the specific needs and preferences of your audience will enable you to create digital products that resonate with them. Conducting market research and creating buyer personas are crucial steps in this process.

Creating Compelling Digital Products

The process of creating compelling digital products involves leveraging your expertise, insights, and creativity to develop valuable assets. Whether it's writing an e-book, designing an online course, or developing software, the focus should be on delivering high-quality and engaging content that provides real value to your audience.

Unleashing Creativity

One of the defining features of selling digital products is its ability to unleash creativity. Digital platforms have democratized entrepreneurship, enabling young minds to showcase their talents and skills. Whether it's creating digital art, designing unique fonts, or composing original music, Gen Z entrepreneurs are finding innovative ways to monetize their passions.

The Power of Niche Markets

Understanding the power of niche markets is crucial for success in the digital product business. Gen Z, known for its diverse interests and values, is driving the demand for highly specialized and personalized digital products. From eco-friendly digital planners to niche gaming apps, catering to specific interests creates a loyal customer base and sets the stage for sustainable growth.

Building a Well-Structured Sales Funnel

A well-structured sales funnel is essential for effectively promoting and selling your digital products. This involves creating compelling sales pages, designing engaging landing pages, and incorporating clear call-to-action buttons to optimize the conversion rate. Testimonials, case studies, and persuasive copy can also be used to enhance the sales process.

Effective Marketing and Promotion Strategies

Marketing and promotion play a vital role in reaching your target audience and driving sales. Implementing effective strategies such as social media marketing, content marketing, and email campaigns can help you maximize the visibility and impact of your digital products.

Optimizing the Customer Experience

Providing a seamless and enjoyable customer experience is key to building a loyal customer base. This involves optimizing the purchasing process, delivering high-quality customer support, and continuously seeking feedback to improve the overall experience.

Data-Driven Decision Making

Utilizing data to make informed decisions is crucial in the digital marketplace. Analyzing key metrics such as conversion rates, customer acquisition costs, and customer lifetime value can provide valuable insights for optimizing your selling strategies.

Social Media as a Catalyst

The seamless integration of social media into the fabric of digital entrepreneurship cannot be overstated. Gen Z, often referred to as the "social media generation," leverages platforms like Instagram, TikTok, and Pinterest to showcase and sell their digital products. The power of influencers in shaping purchasing decisions among Gen Z cannot be ignored, making social media a potent catalyst for digital product sales.

Economic Empowerment

Selling digital products empowers Gen Z to take control of their financial destinies. The gig economy, characterized by short-term and freelance work, is thriving, and digital product sales play a significant role in this economic paradigm shift. With low entry barriers and minimal overhead costs, Gen Z entrepreneurs can turn their digital creations into profitable ventures, fostering financial independence.

Evolving in the Digital Marketplace

The digital marketplace is constantly evolving, and it's important to stay adaptable and innovative. Keeping up with the latest trends, technologies, and consumer behaviors will enable you to continuously refine and expand your digital product offerings.

The Future of Digital Entrepreneurship

As we peer into the future, the trajectory of selling digital products for Gen Z seems boundless. Rapid advancements in technology, coupled with an ever-evolving digital landscape, open new avenues for innovation and growth. The adaptability of Gen Z to emerging trends, combined with their inherent tech-savvy nature, positions them as the driving force behind the continued evolution of digital entrepreneurship.

The world of selling digital products offers a wealth of opportunities for individuals to monetize their expertise and creativity. By following the strategies outlined in this chapter and staying committed to delivering value to your audience, you can build a successful and sustainable business in the digital realm.

Remember, the key to success lies in understanding your audience, creating compelling products, and implementing effective marketing and sales strategies. Embrace the digital age and unleash your potential in the exciting world of selling digital products.

Creating Digital Products

Creating digital products is a great way to start making money online. It can feel overwhelming to decide where to start, what should be in it, and what the end product should look like. However, it does not have to be complicated or include all the bells and whistles. In fact, sometimes it's better if it doesn't because you don't want to include anything in there that doesn't solve one specific problem or solution.

Here are some steps to get started with your general digital product idea:

1. Determine the desired destination and the most common starting place.

2. Decide on the best way to solve the problem or provide the solution.

3. Create a summary of everything you still need to create, including tools, teaching materials, and anything else you'll be including.

If you're creating an eBook or digital course, outline the different chapters or modules you'll want to cover. You can always then go back to your audience and talk more about what you're planning on covering. If you're creating a preset, stock photo collection, or a creative template, you might want to plan out what will be in that collection and put together a PDF thanking your customer for their purchase as well as some instructions on how to use it.

Once you've settled on an idea for your next (or first) digital product, it's time to get to creating it. In this step of the process, there is a simple 4-part process that'll take you from idea to done and help you end up with a digital product. The process includes:

1. Brainstorming and outlining your product.

2. Creating your product.

3. Polishing and refining your product.

4. Launching and promoting your product.

Pricing Your Digital Product

Pricing digital products can be tricky, but there are several strategies to consider. One common strategy is cost-based pricing, which sets prices based on the production and distribution costs associated with creating digital products. However, it's important to also consider the value of the product to the customer and the profit you want to make. You can also use competitor-based pricing, where you research your competitors' prices and set your own accordingly. Another strategy is value-based pricing, where you price your digital products according to their perceived value to the customer. This can involve conducting customer research and emphasizing the benefits of your product. It's also important to test different pricing strategies and adjust as needed. Ultimately, the pricing decisions you make should be based on your company goals and beliefs.

Benefits of selling digital products over physical products:

Lower overhead costs: Digital products have lower production and storage costs, resulting in higher profit margins.

Global reach: The internet allows you to reach a vast audience without geographical limitations.

Lower barriers to entry: Creating digital products requires less upfront investment compared to physical products.

Scalability: Digital products can be created once and sold repeatedly, generating passive income.

Flexibility: Digital products can be easily updated and delivered to customers, ensuring they remain relevant and valuable.

Accessibility: Digital products can be more accessible to customers, as they can be downloaded or accessed instantly.

Chapter IV

Becoming a Reseller

Become an e-Commmerce Tycoon Using Your Business Instincts

Reselling is a lucrative business that allows you to turn your passion for fashion, tech gadgets, or vintage collectibles into a thriving venture. In this chapter, we will explore the ins and outs of becoming a reseller, navigating the digital marketplace, and using social media to carve your niche.

Entrepreneurship is thriving among Gen Z, who seek financial independence, creative expression, and meaningful connections. Reselling is a popular avenue for transforming product passions into a lucrative business. The online platforms have made reselling a global phenomenon, with the global resale market projected to reach $64 billion by 2025.

Understanding the Reseller Business

The reseller business model involves purchasing products from manufacturers, liquidators, or other retailers and then selling them to your own customers. This approach allows individuals to enter the e-commerce space without the need to create their own products, making it an attractive option for those seeking low-barrier entry into entrepreneurship.

The Reseller's Journey: Getting Started

To embark on your reselling journey, it's essential to understand the various types of reselling models and determine the right fit for your entrepreneurial aspirations. Whether you choose to operate as a traditional reseller, or dropshipper, or adopt a subscription-based model, each approach offers unique advantages and considerations.

The Power of Your Passion: Turning Hobbies into Income

One of the most compelling aspects of the reselling business is the ability to turn your passion into a lucrative income stream. Whether it's limited edition sneakers, vintage vinyl records, or handmade crafts, your unique taste can be the key to a successful reselling venture. In fact, a survey by Etsy reveals that 97% of sellers on their platform consider their Etsy shop a business, with 77% running their shops from their homes. (Source: Etsy - Seller survey insights)

Navigating the Digital Marketplace: From eBay to Niche Platforms

The digital marketplace has democratized the reselling game. Platforms like eBay, Poshmark, and Depop have become virtual storefronts for resellers to showcase their products to a global audience. However, success lies in finding the right platform for your niche. For instance, if you're into vintage clothing, Depop might be your go-to, while tech gadgets may find a thriving market on eBay.

Social Media: Your Ultimate Ally

The power of social media cannot be overstated in the reselling world. Instagram, TikTok, and Pinterest are not just platforms for sharing cat videos or dance challenges; they are powerful marketing tools. A study by Hootsuite reveals that Instagram's potential advertising reach is estimated to be over 1.16 billion users. Utilize these platforms to build a brand, connect with potential buyers, and showcase the personality behind your reselling business. (Source: Hootsuite - Instagram advertising reach)

The Sustainable Edge: Eco-friendly Entrepreneurship

Gen Z is spearheading the charge towards sustainable practices, and reselling aligns perfectly with this ethos. By giving pre-loved items a new lease on life, resellers contribute to the circular economy, reducing waste and promoting sustainable consumption. A Nielsen study found that 73% of global consumers say they would change their consumption habits to reduce their impact on the environment. (Source: Nielsen - Global consumers' sustainability survey)

Overcoming Challenges: The Resilient Reseller

While the reselling business offers immense opportunities, it's not without its challenges. From dealing with fluctuating market trends to navigating shipping logistics, resilience is the key to success. Learning from setbacks, adapting to market shifts, and embracing a continuous learning mindset will set you apart in this competitive arena.

The Power of Marketing in Reselling

Effective marketing is a cornerstone of success in the reselling business. By leveraging social media, content marketing, and other digital strategies, resellers can attract and engage their target audience, ultimately driving sales and fostering brand loyalty. This chapter will explore the art of compelling storytelling and the science of data-driven marketing to help you elevate your reselling business.

Benefits of Reselling: A Path to Entrepreneurial Freedom

Think of reselling as your gateway to freedom. You define your niche, source your treasures, and sculpt your ideal customer experience. It's a business model that scales with your ambition, offering sustainable income and endless possibilities for growth. Whether you're a tech-savvy millennial or a creative visionary, the reselling world welcomes you with open arms (and an endless inventory!).

But freedom doesn't come without some groundwork. This chapter will equip you with the knowledge and best practices to navigate the dynamic reselling landscape. We'll dive into the art of effective marketing, explore the nuances of different selling platforms, and unveil the secrets to building a thriving online business.

As you navigate the reseller's journey, remember that the e-commerce landscape is ever-evolving. By remaining adaptable, embracing creativity, and staying attuned to the needs of your audience, you can build a thriving reselling business that stands the test of time.

Best of luck on your reselling adventure!

Chapter V

Affiliate Marketing

The Hustle Hackers Guide to Affiliate Marketing

Forget side hustles. Forget internships. Buckle up, Gen Z, because we're about to crack the code of a money-making machine that lets you be your own boss, curate your passions, and build an empire from your phone. Welcome to the wild world of Affiliate Marketing, where influence meets income, and your social media cred transforms into cold, hard cash.

Think of yourself as a digital Robin Hood, except instead of stealing from the rich, you're siphoning off affiliate links like Robinhood-level archery. You recommend awesome products, and brands you genuinely love, and every time someone clicks your link and buys, you get a sweet commission. It's like getting paid to rave about your favorite stuff, only better - because here, the rave comes with a paycheck.

And yes, before you ask, it's **TOTALLY LEGIT!** Companies all over the world are throwing money at creative minds like you to spread the word about their products. And why wouldn't they? Gen Z, you're the most digitally savvy, socially conscious generation ever. You control the zeitgeist, and your thumbs hold the power to launch trends like rockets. Brands want a piece of that pie, and affiliate marketing is your VIP pass to the table.

But wait, there's more! Affiliate marketing isn't just about making bank (although let's be honest, that's pretty darn awesome). It's about freedom. Freedom to choose your niche, whether it's sustainable fashion, the hottest tech gadgets, or even dank memes (yes, seriously). It's about building a community around your passions, connecting with like-minded hustlers, and becoming a trusted voice in your online space. It's about ditching the 9-to-5 grind and crafting a career that's as unique and vibrant as you are.

Sounds too good to be true? Think again. Here's a taste of the affiliate marketing magic:

19-year-old Sarah turned her love for vegan makeup into a thriving Instagram account, landing sweet deals with cruelty-free brands and earning enough to ditch college and travel the world.

Josh, a college dropout gamer, built a YouTube channel reviewing retro consoles, racking up millions of views and securing affiliate partnerships with gaming giants, all while rocking his pajamas.

The "Meme Lord" himself, a high school senior with a knack for internet humor, used affiliate links in his viral posts, turning his online jokes into a six-figure income before prom night.

These aren't fairy tales, folks. These are real Gen Zers rewriting the rules of the game. And you, yes you, can be next. So, ditch the boring work, put down the resume, and grab your phone. It's time to level up your hustle game and become the boss of your destiny. Welcome to the affiliate marketing revolution, Gen Z. Let's get this party started.

Niche or Bust: Finding Your Golden Egg in the Affiliate Jungle

Remember that the delicious feeling of stumbling upon the perfect meme, the one that perfectly captures your soul's existential angst? Yeah, finding your affiliate marketing niche is kinda like that – but with the added bonus of cold, hard cash raining down upon you. In this chapter, we'll crack open the treasure chest of niches and help you unearth your golden egg.

First things first: forget the "get-rich-quick" schemes. Building a successful affiliate empire takes time, effort, and, yes, you guessed it, knowing your stuff. So, step one: **dive deep into your passions**. What makes your heart sing? What do you geek out about until 3 AM? Is it K-pop dance routines, sustainable gardening hacks, or mastering the art of sourdough bread? Whatever it is, that's your starting point.

But passion alone isn't enough. We need to make sure there's gold in those hills, folks.

Here's how to validate your niche:

Market research: Google is like a detective. Check forums, social media groups, and even niche subreddits dedicated to your interests. Is there a thriving community? Are people actively talking about and buying things related to your niche?

Competition check: Scope out the competition. Are there established affiliate players in your space? Don't worry, competition isn't a dead end, it's a map. Learn from their strengths and weaknesses, then carve your unique path.

Affiliate program availability: This is where the rubber meets the road. Do brands in your niche offer affiliate programs? Check out affiliate networks like CJ Affiliate, ShareASale, or Impact Radius. You'd be surprised by the hidden gems you might find.

Found your niche? Awesome! Now let's tailor it to your Gen Z superpowers. Remember, you're not just another affiliate, you're a **social media ninja, a content creation sensei, and a trendsetting trailblazer.**

Here's how to rock your niche with a Gen Z twist:

Authenticity is your armor: Be real, be relatable, be you. Gen Z can sniff out a fake from a mile away. Share your genuine experiences, struggles, and successes. Let your personality shine through, and don't be afraid to be quirky (it's kinda your birthright, after all).

Content is king (or queen): Master the art of storytelling. Whether it's hilarious TikTok reviews, eye-catching Instagram stories, or in-depth YouTube tutorials, create content that engages your audience and showcases your expertise. Remember, you're not just selling products, you're building a community.

Embrace the platforms you love: Don't try to be everywhere at once. Focus on the platforms where your target audience hangs out. Are they on Twitch streaming their gaming exploits? Join them! Are they obsessed with Twitter threads? Get your voice heard! Tailor your content and engagement to where your peeps are already vibing.

Remember, finding your niche and building your brand takes time and experimentation.

Don't be afraid to pivot, refine, and adapt. The key is to stay passionate, learn from your failures, and keep creating content that resonates with your tribe. So, go forth! Explore the jungle of niches, discover your golden egg, and build a kingdom that reflects your unique voice and passions. The world is your oyster (or maybe your sourdough starter, if that's your jam). Now go forth and conquer!

Check out tools like **Buzzsumo** or **Ahrefs** to identify trending topics and content gaps in your niche. This can be your secret weapon for creating fresh, engaging content that attracts an audience and drives those sweet, sweet clicks.

Platform Playground: Where Your Affiliate Empire Takes Flight

Hold onto your hype wigs, Gen Z, because we're about to launch your affiliate rocket ship into the stratosphere of social media! This chapter is all about mastering the platforms that will transform your clicks into clinking coins. Buckle up, because it's time to take flight!

#1: Instagram – The Curated Canvas of Cool:

Think of Instagram as the runway for your brand. Craft aesthetically pleasing posts that showcase your niche expertise. Whether it's flat-lay fashion shots, drool-worthy food pics, or mind-blowing tech unboxings, make them visually captivating and on-brand. Use

Stories and Reels to offer behind-the-scenes glimpses, live tutorials, and engaging Q&A sessions. Remember, Gen Z craves authenticity, so show your personality and let your love for your niche shine through.

Pro Tip: Leverage Instagram's shoppable posts feature to link directly to affiliate products. Make it seamless for your followers to go from "like" to "buy" in a single click.

#2: YouTube – The Educational Playground:

Turn your knowledge into captivating content on YouTube. Create in-depth tutorials, product reviews, and entertaining explainers that showcase your expertise. Engage with your viewers through comments and respond to questions. Remember, Gen Z values authenticity and humor, so don't be afraid to inject your personality and sprinkle in some memes for good measure.

Pro Tip: Collaborate with other YouTubers in your niche for cross-promotion and audience expansion. Tag relevant brands in your videos and consider incorporating sponsored content deals as you grow your channel.

#3: TikTok – The Trendsetting Tornado:

If you haven't mastered the art of the viral TikTok dance, now's the time to brush up on your moves. This platform is all about short, snappy, and engaging content. Get creative with transitions, challenges, and trending sounds to capture attention and showcase your affiliate products in a fun and memorable way. Partner with micro-influencers in your niche for collaborative TikTok challenges and boost your reach.

Pro Tip: Utilize TikTok's affiliate marketing tools to seamlessly integrate product links into your videos. Don't forget the power of hashtags – research trending hashtags within your niche and use them strategically to get discovered.

#4: Twitch – The Gaming Oasis:

For the streamer squad, Twitch is your battlefield. Share your gaming expertise, review new releases, and showcase sponsored products organically while you dominate the virtual arena. Engage with your viewers through chat and build a loyal community around your shared passion. Don't be afraid to get silly and have fun – Gen Z appreciates authenticity and genuine enthusiasm.

Pro Tip: Collaborate with other streamers in your niche for co-op campaigns and cross-promotion. Consider offering exclusive discounts or early access to affiliate products for your dedicated Twitch community.

Remember, mastering any platform takes practice and experimentation. Don't be afraid to try new things, analyze your results, and adapt your strategy. The key is to find your voice, engage your audience, and showcase your affiliate products in a way that resonates with your Gen Z tribe.

Content Craft: Weaving Words that Convert Clicks into Cash

Okay, let's get down to the nitty-gritty: crafting content that turns those clicks into cold, hard cash. Remember, words are your weapons, and your audience is the target. In this chapter, we'll sharpen your copywriting skills and transform you into content creation ninjas, ready to dominate the digital battlefield.

know your audience. What makes them tick? What are their pain points? What kind of language do they resonate with? Dive deep into their online hangouts, analyze their comments, and listen to their conversations. Remember, you're not just selling products, you're solving problems and fulfilling desires.

Now, let's weave some magic with words:

Headlines that hook: Your headline is like the gateway drug to your content. Make it irresistible, attention-grabbing, and packed with intrigue. Use powerful words, ask questions, and tap into your audience's curiosity. Think "5 Sustainable Hacks to Level Up Your Eco-Kitchen" or "Unlock Your Inner Gamer: The Ultimate Tech Setup Guide."

Storytelling that captivates: People connect with stories. Weave a narrative around your product that showcases its benefits and resonates with your audience's desires. Let them visualize themselves using the product, achieving their goals, and living their best lives. Think relatable anecdotes, personal experiences, and even a dash of humor to keep them hooked.

Benefits, not features: Ditch the boring product specs and focus on the "why." What makes this product life-changing? How will it solve their problems and make their lives better? Highlight the emotional benefits alongside the practical ones. Remember, people buy feelings, not features.

Calls to action that convert: Don't leave your audience hanging. Tell them exactly what you want them to do. Use clear, concise CTAs like "Shop Now and Save 15%" or "Click Here to Download Your Free Guide." Make it easy for them to take the next step towards affiliate bliss.

Remember, visuals are your allies. Eye-catching images, infographics, and even short videos can break up your text and add a layer of engagement. Use high-quality visuals that complement your content and showcase your affiliate products in their best light.

Bonus tip: Experiment with different content formats. Blog posts, listicles, quizzes, product reviews, and video tutorials – the possibilities are endless. Find what resonates best with your audience and keep them coming back for more.

Mastering the art of content creation takes time and practice. Don't be afraid to experiment, analyze your results, and adapt your strategy. The key is to find your voice, connect with your audience, and weave words that compel them to click, buy, and become loyal fans of your affiliate empire.

Chapter VI

Becoming an Influencer

Own Your Fame in the Age of Likes

It's time to rewrite the rules of success. Forget the cubicle grind, the endless meetings, and the fluorescent-lit soul-suck. Your currency isn't some dusty degree, it's raw charisma, killer content, and a legion of followers who hang on your every word (or meme, or perfectly winged eyeliner tutorial). Welcome to the age of the influencer, where your bedroom can be your boardroom, your passions your paycheck, and your voice the soundtrack to millions.

But wait, isn't being an influencer just, like, taking selfies and getting free stuff?

Hold up. This ain't your parent's idea of fame. Influencing, at its core, is about _building a community_. You're the curator, the hype-man, the BFF who spills the real tea on sustainable sneakers, the fire escape route outta the soul-crushing 9-to-5. You're the pied piper of trends, the Yoda of niche obsessions, the Michelangelo of cat eyeliner. People trust you, listen to you, and wanna rock the same neon socks you do. That's power, Gen Z. Real, digital-age power. **And the numbers back it up**. The influencer marketing game is hotter than Sriracha on pizza. Brands are throwing shade (and Benjamins) at creators like you, desperate to tap into your authentic voice and reach. By 2025, the influencer marketing industry is expected to hit a cool **$23.7 billion**. That's more than enough cheddar to ditch the ramen and live large, all while doing what you love.

But don't get blinded by the dollar signs. Influencing is a marathon, not a sprint. It's about hustle, heart, and serious #contentgame. You gotta find your niche, your tribe, your voice that cuts through the endless scroll.

Think of it like building your own empire, one perfectly-lit Instagram post at a time. You're the CEO, the creative director, the hype-woman-in-chief. You curate your brand, tell your story, and captivate your audience. It's not just about selfies and sponsorships, it's about building something real, something that resonates, something that makes you wanna scream, "This is me, and this is **my** world!"

So, are you ready to ditch the ordinary and become the influencer extraordinaire? Buckle up, Gen Z, because this chapter is your roadmap to online fame (and fortune). We'll dive deep into the nitty-gritty of finding your niche, crafting killer content, building your community, and navigating the ever-changing world of social media. We'll bust myths, expose the influencer secrets, and show you how to turn your passions into a paycheck (and maybe even snag some free swag along the way).

This ain't just a chapter, it's a manifesto. It's a battle cry for the generation that rewrites the rules, flips the script, and dances to its own damn beat. So grab your phone, unleash your inner rockstar, and get ready to own your story. The influencer age is yours for the taking. Let's do this!

Niche Down, Slay Up: Unearthing Your Golden Content Mine

Yo, influencer FAM! Remember that empire you're building? Well, it all starts with a rock-solid foundation. And that foundation, my friends, is your niche. It's your secret sauce, your claim to internet fame, the gravitational pull that keeps your audience glued to your screen like pizza to a hungry teenager.

But what if you're lost in a sea of "aesthetic" and "travel blogger wannabes"? Don't fret, Gen Z. Unearthing your niche is like unearthing buried treasure – it takes a little digging, but the reward is pure gold (or, you know, social media clout, which is pretty shiny too).

Here's the drill:

Dive deep into your passions. What makes your soul sing? Skateboarding? Sustainable fashion? Astrophysics explained in memes? Own that weirdness! The more passionate you are, the more authentic your content, and the more likely you are to attract a tribe who shares your vibe.

Think micro, not macro. Forget the generic "lifestyle" influencer tag. Be the queen of vegan baking, the king of historical reenactments, or the Yoda of ASMR slime tutorials. The more specific your niche, the more dedicated your following will be.

Do your research. See who's already slaying it in your niche. Analyze their content, see what resonates, and then find your own unique angle. Be the David to their Goliath, the sriracha to their ketchup.

Remember, your niche is your playground. It's where you can experiment, express yourself, and build a community that feels like home. So, don't be afraid to get weird, get specific, and get personal.

Now, let's talk about the good stuff: content! Because once you've unearthed your niche, it's time to let your creativity run wild. But before you hit record on that next TikTok dance challenge, remember these golden nuggets:

Quality over quantity. One killer video that showcases your passion and expertise is worth ten shaky selfies. Invest in good lighting, sound, and editing software. Your audience deserves the royal treatment, even if your set is still your bedroom.

Storytelling is key. Weave your niche into everything you do. Tell the story behind your love for vintage cameras, the struggles of mastering a new skateboard trick, and the science behind that perfect sourdough starter. People connect with stories, so make yours epic.

Be authentically you. Ditch the filters, the fake brags, and the forced trends. Your audience can smell inauthenticity from a mile away. Be real, be vulnerable, and be unapologetically you. That's what makes you stand out from the crowd.

And don't forget the power of collaboration! Team up with other creators in your niche, do challenges, host live streams, and bounce ideas off each other. It's a great way to expand your reach, learn new skills, and keep your content fresh.

Remember, building a successful influencer empire takes time, dedication, and a whole lot of heart. But with the right niche, killer content, and a sprinkle of collaboration, you'll be slaying the influencer game in no time. So, go forth, Gen Z, and unearth your golden content mine! The world awaits your unique brand of awesome.

Bonus Tip: Don't be afraid to experiment with different platforms! While Instagram might be your current jam, TikTok could be your next goldmine. Explore, adapt, and conquer the ever-changing social media landscape.

Community Alchemy: Turning Followers into Family

Think of your online space as a campfire. You're the storyteller, the hype-man, the one roasting marshmallows (metaphorically, of course. Fire safety, people!). But a lonely campfire ain't much fun. You need marshmallows to share, stories to swap, and laughter that echoes through the digital night. That's where your community comes in.

But how do you turn a bunch of followers into a ride-or-die fam? Well, buckle up, because we're about to drop some serious community alchemy knowledge:

1. Engagement is your love potion: Likes are cool, and comments are hotter. Respond to messages, answer questions, and participate in discussions. Show your followers you actually care about what they have to say. Run polls, ask for opinions and host Q&A sessions. Make them feel like they're not just watching a show, they're part of the backstage crew.

2. Foster a sense of belonging: Create hashtags for your community, run challenges they can participate in, share inside jokes, and celebrate their achievements. Make them feel like they're part of a club, a secret society, a tribe of like-minded weirdos.

3. Get personal, but keep it real: Show glimpses of your life beyond the perfectly curated feed. Share struggles, vulnerabilities, and triumphs. Let your followers see the human behind the brand. Remember, authenticity is the ultimate aphrodisiac for online relationships.

4. Embrace the power of stories: People don't just want facts, they want feels. Use your platform to tell stories that inspire, educate, and entertain. Share your journey, your passions, and your struggles. Make your followers laugh, cry, and everything in between.

5. Give back to the community: Remember, it's a two-way street. Support other creators in your niche, promote small businesses you love, and advocate for causes you care about. Show your followers that you're not just in it for the likes, you're in it to make a difference.

And don't forget the power of platforms! Each one has its own unique vibe and engagement style.

Instagram: Master the art of the perfect caption, utilize Stories for behind-the-scenes glimpses, and tap into Reels and IGTV for longer-form content.

TikTok: Embrace the trends, get creative with edits, and join challenges to go viral. Remember, it's all about short, punchy, and entertaining content.

YouTube: Build a channel that showcases your expertise, personality, and storytelling skills. Live streams and collaborations are your friends here.

Twitter: Be witty, be insightful, be part of the conversation. Use threads to tell longer stories and engage in real-time debates.

Building a strong community takes time and effort, but the rewards are priceless.

A loyal following will not only boost your engagement and reach, but they'll also become your cheerleaders, your collaborators, and your friends. They'll be the ones sharing your content, defending you against trolls, and celebrating your every win.

Remember, **your community is your superpower.** Nurture it, cherish it, and watch it grow. Together, you can create something truly awesome in the digital world. So, go forth, influencer FAM, and spread the love! And hey, if you have any killer community-building tips, drop them in the comments below. Let's share the knowledge and watch our online tribes thrive!

Bonus Tip: Don't be afraid to get creative! Host online game nights, organize virtual charity events or even start a book club for your niche. The possibilities are endless!

Mastering the Art of Partnerships and Sponsorships

Think of it like scaling Mount Influencer. You've reached base camp (building your community), and honed your climbing skills (content creation), and now it's time to navigate the treacherous terrain of brand collaborations. But fear not, fam! With the right approach, you can reach the summit of sponsor-fueled success.

First, Know your worth: You're not just a walking billboard, you're a creative powerhouse with a loyal following. Don't undervalue yourself! Research industry rates, analyze your engagement metrics, and be confident in your negotiation skills. Remember, you bring something unique to the table, and brands should be willing to pay for it.

Second, be picky about your partners: Don't just sell out to the highest bidder. Align yourself with brands that resonate with your niche, your values, and your audience. Partnering with a brand that clashes with your vibe is a recipe for disaster (and potentially lost followers).

Now, let's explore the partnership landscape

Sponsored posts: The bread and butter of influencer marketing. Create content (photos, videos, stories) promoting a brand or product. Be transparent by using hashtags like #ad or #spon. Authenticity is key here!

Brand ambassador: Build a long-term relationship with a brand, representing them at events, creating exclusive content, and advocating for their products. Think of yourself as their digital BFF.

Product development: Collaborate with brands to create products your audience will love. Put your unique spin on their offerings and watch the sales roll in.

Affiliate marketing: Earn a commission through sales generated by your unique referral link or code. Think of it as getting paid for spreading the word about your favorite stuff.

Remember, successful partnerships are win-win scenarios. The brand gets access to your engaged audience, and you get paid to do what you love (and maybe snag some cool free stuff along the way).

Here are some bonus tips for landing killer partnerships

Network like nobody's business: Attend industry events, connect with brands on social media, and don't be afraid to reach out directly. Remember, the squeaky wheel gets the grease (and the sponsorships).

Build a killer media kit: Showcase your stats, demographics, and audience engagement in a visually appealing format. Think of it as your influencer resume.

Stay professional and organized: Deliver content on time, communicate clearly with brands, and keep up with your contractual obligations. Remember, your reputation is everything in the influencer world.

Mastering the art of partnerships and sponsorships takes time and effort, but the rewards are sweet. You can build a sustainable career, support brands you love, and all while doing what you do best: connecting with your awesome community. So go forth, influencer fam, and conquer the mountain of influencer partnerships!

Chapter VII

Dropshipping

Hack the Hype for the Trend-Obsessed Gen Z

The future of work is remote, the currency is clout, and the hustle is all about riding the wave of what's hot. In this digital gold rush, there's no quicker path to building your own empire than mastering the art of the **dropship trending product business**. Think of it as your personal hype train, fueled by TikTok virality, Instagram aesthetics, and a smidge of entrepreneurial genius. Buckle up, because we're about to drop some knowledge hotter than a freshly minted meme.

Dropshipping is an e-commerce business model where you, the seller, act as a middleman between the customer and the supplier. No more dusty warehouses or overflowing garages! Here's the lowdown on how it works:

You curate: Think of yourself as a digital trend DJ, spinning the hottest products on the algorithm. You research, choose, and list trending items like fidget spinners, holographic phone cases, or whatever the next viral gadget might be. Your online store becomes your virtual storefront, showcasing the coolest finds without you ever needing to touch them.

They buy: A customer spots a must-have item on your site and hits "buy." This is where the magic happens. Instead of you shipping the product, the order gets automatically forwarded to your supplier.

Supplier ships: The supplier, who actually holds the inventory, packs and ships the product directly to your customer. You act as the facilitator, the orchestrator of this e-commerce symphony.

Profiting from the hype: Here's the part that makes your hustle heart sing. You set the price for the product, factoring in the supplier's cost and your desired profit margin. When the customer completes their purchase, the difference between your selling price and the supplier's cost lands in your pocket. The higher the demand for the product, the more loot you rake in!

Why Dropping is Dope

First, let's ditch the stuffy business jargon. Dropshipping isn't your grandpa's brick-and-mortar hustle. It's the ultimate side hustle for the side-eye generation. You, the trend whisperer, the master of the scroll, curate the hottest products. Think fidget spinners in 2017, holographic phone cases last week, and who knows what mind-bending gadget will explode next? You don't hold any inventory, you're basically a hype DJ spinning the latest tracks on the algorithm. When someone buys from your online store, your supplier ships it directly to them. You're the curator, the connector, the trend kingpin, without the pesky warehouse overhead.

Low startup costs: No need for hefty inventory investments. You can launch your business with a laptop and an internet connection.

Scalability: Adapt your offerings to trending products easily, adjusting your inventory in real-time based on demand.

Location independence: Run your business from anywhere with a Wi-Fi signal, whether it's your bedroom, a cozy coffee shop, or a beachside hammock.

Flexibility: Manage your time on your own terms. Dropshipping can be a side hustle or a full-time gig, depending on your goals and dedication.

Data Dropping

Here's a stat to make your hustle heart sing: the global dropshipping market is projected to hit a cool **$557.9 billion by 2025**. That's more money than Elon Musk's spare change jar. And guess who's driving this trend? You, the meme-loving, trend-spotting Gen Z. Your buying power is real, and your fingers are glued to screens that constantly bombard you with the next must-have item. You're not just consumers, you're trendsetters, and dropshipping lets you capitalize on your own cultural currency.

Storytelling Sells

But it's not just about the latest gadget. Remember, you're the curator, the storyteller. Craft a brand that speaks your tribe's lingo. Ditch the corporate suits and embrace the memes, the inside jokes, the shared experiences. Build a community around your brand, not just a store. Let your customers feel like they're part of the exclusive hype fam, the trend detectives uncovering the next big thing before it goes mainstream.

The Hustle is Real

Look, it's not all avocado toast and viral dances. Running a dropship business takes work. You gotta research trends like a hawk, negotiate with suppliers like a diplomat, and market your brand like a social media ninja. But here's the beauty: you can do it all from your bedroom, fueled by ramen and the sweet dopamine rush of a sale notification.

Competition: The dropshipping world is bustling, so finding unique products and standing out is crucial.

Marketing hustle: You need to drive traffic to your store and convince customers to buy from you, not your competitors.

Profit margins: Dropshipping profits can be lower than traditional retail models, especially for low-priced items.

Supplier dependence: Your success hinges on reliable suppliers with good quality products and efficient shipping.

The Dropship Dream

Dropshipping ain't just a business, it's a lifestyle. It's about turning your trend obsession into a side hustle that pays for your next Coachella trip, your dream tech setup, or even that down payment on a Mars condo (Elon wouldn't judge). This is your chance to hack the system, bend the rules, and prove that the future belongs to the nimble, the trend-savvy, and the dropshipping masters of Gen Z.

The next viral sensation could be lurking just one scroll away. Now go forth, young entrepreneurs, and build your hype-fueled empires. Just don't forget to document your journey with fire selfies and killer hashtags. The world is your oyster (or maybe your avocado toast?), and the dropship hype train is waiting for you. All aboard!

Building a Booming Dropshipping Business: Your Guide to E-commerce Success

1. Niche Down, Don't Drown

Forget the "general store" approach. The dropshipping landscape is teeming with competition. To stand out, you need to specialize. Find a niche, a specific market segment with passionate customers and unmet needs. Think yoga accessories for eco-conscious athletes, or cat toys designed by feline behaviorists. The more targeted your niche, the easier it is to attract a loyal following and build brand authority.

2. Source Savvy

Your dropshipping suppliers are the backbone of your business. Choose reliable partners who offer high-quality products, competitive pricing, and efficient fulfillment. Research extensively, compare options, and prioritize suppliers with transparent communication and a proven track record. Remember, your reputation is on the line with every order, so choose suppliers who share your commitment to customer satisfaction.

3. Craft Your Online Haven

Your website is your digital storefront, the first impression you make on potential customers. Invest in a user-friendly platform, prioritize clear product descriptions and high-quality images, and ensure a seamless checkout process. Remember, mobile responsiveness is crucial in today's digital landscape. Your website should be an extension of your brand, reflecting your unique voice and values.

4. Marketing Magic

Building an audience takes effort. Leverage social media platforms like Instagram and TikTok to showcase your products and engage with your target audience. Utilize targeted ads, influencer collaborations, and organic content marketing to drive traffic to your store. Remember, email marketing remains a powerful tool for nurturing leads and building customer loyalty.

5. Customer Centricity

In the dropshipping world, exceptional customer service is your golden ticket. Respond promptly to inquiries, address concerns efficiently, and go the extra mile to exceed expectations. Building trust and positive relationships with your customers is the foundation of long-term success. Remember, happy customers become brand advocates, spreading the word and fueling your business growth.

Beyond the Basics

Now, let's delve deeper into some strategic considerations to optimize your dropshipping journey:

Branding is King: Develop a strong brand identity that resonates with your niche. Your logo, colors, and messaging should all work together to tell your unique story and differentiate you from the competition.

Data-Driven Decisions: Track your website traffic, conversion rates, and customer behavior using analytics tools. Use this data to identify areas for improvement, optimize your marketing campaigns, and refine your product offerings.

Embrace Automation: Utilize tools and software to automate repetitive tasks like order processing and email marketing. This frees up your time to focus on more strategic initiatives like product development and customer engagement.

Stay Agile and Adaptable: The e-commerce landscape is constantly evolving. Be prepared to adjust your strategies, experiment with new tactics, and stay ahead of the curve to maintain your competitive edge.

Bonus Tip: Consider offering value-added services like gift wrapping or personalized notes to differentiate yourself from competitors and enhance the customer experience.

Conquering the Conversion Conundrum: Mastering the Checkout and Beyond

You've laid the groundwork. You've found your niche, partnered with reliable suppliers, and crafted a captivating online store. Now, the real magic happens – transforming curious onlookers into loyal customers. This chapter focuses on the crucial art of conversion optimization, dissecting the checkout process and revealing tactics to turn browsers into buyers.

Frictionless Flow: Imagine a checkout process smooth as silk, guiding customers with intuitive steps and eliminating any hint of hesitation. Optimize every stage:

Clear Calls to Action: Don't make your customers hunt for the Buy button. Place it prominently throughout the product pages and cart.

Guest Checkout Option: Not everyone wants to create an account. Offer a quick guest checkout option for effortless transactions.

Multiple Payment Gateways: Cater to diverse preferences. Provide a variety of secure payment options, including popular digital wallets.

Transparent Shipping Costs: Hide no surprises. Display shipping costs upfront, and consider offering free shipping options to sweeten the deal.

Mobile Optimization: Remember, many browse and buy on their phones. Ensure your checkout experience is flawless on mobile devices.

The Power of Persuasion: A well-designed checkout page isn't just functional, it's persuasive. Employ subtle nudges to inspire confidence and encourage action:

Social Proof: Showcase customer testimonials and positive reviews to build trust and showcase the value of your products.

Scarcity Signals: Use limited-time offers or limited-stock indicators to create a sense of urgency and prompt conversions.

Upselling and Cross-selling: Recommend complementary products to increase order value without feeling pushy. Offer bundles or curated sets to present a compelling value proposition.

Live Chat Support: Address concerns and answer questions in real time. Live chat offers a human touch and can alleviate checkout anxieties.

3. Beyond the Buy Button: The journey doesn't end with a completed order. Nurture customer relationships and encourage repeat purchases:

Order Tracking and Updates: Keep customers informed every step of the way, from order confirmation to delivery. Transparency builds trust and reduces anxiety.

Post-Purchase: Send personalized emails thanking customers for their purchase and asking for feedback. Offer exclusive discounts or early access to new products to incentivize future purchases.

Loyalty Programs: Reward repeat customers with points, discounts, or exclusive benefits. Loyalty programs encourage long-term engagement and build brand advocates.

Remember: Data is your ally. Track conversion rates, analyze abandoned carts, and A/B test different checkout elements to identify areas for improvement. Continuously refine your process based on real-world data to maximize your conversion magic.

Bonus Tip: Offer a "Save for Later" option to capture hesitant customers and nurture them with targeted email campaigns later.

Mastering the checkout is an ongoing process, but with these strategies and a data-driven approach, you can turn hesitant visitors into happy customers, fueling the growth of your dropshipping empire. In the next chapter, we'll explore the thrilling world of paid advertising, a powerful tool to amplify your reach and attract new customers to your e-commerce haven.

Chapter VIII

Build a YouTube Channel

From Bedroom Studio to Billion-View Boss

Ever felt like your phone screen pulsates with unrealized potential? Like your memes deserve a global stage, your gameplays a stadium roar, and your DIY hacks a Nobel Prize (okay, maybe just a shoutout from Buzzfeed)? Welcome to the club, Generation Hustle. This ain't your grandparents' lemonade stand – this is the YouTube kingdom, where internet stardom is just a click, edit, and upload away.

Picture this: your bedroom morphs into a buzzing studio, fueled by caffeine and creativity. You're the CEO, the director, the editor, the meme lord, all rolled into one. Your laptop hums with the symphony of your hustle, churning out videos that captivate millions, igniting laughter, and maybe even sparking a social revolution (who knows, you might be the next Greta Thunberg, but with way cooler dance moves).

But hold your horses, aspiring mogul. YouTube glory isn't a microwaveable burrito – it takes dedication, strategy, and a sprinkle of viral magic. This chapter is your cheat sheet, your roadmap from bedroom broadcaster to monetized mastermind. We'll crack the code, bust the myths, and unveil the secrets to turning your YouTube passion into a cash-flowing empire.

First things first: **ditch the "get rich quick" schemes.** Sustainable success takes time, sweat, and a boatload of creativity. But hey, that's where you shine, right? You're the generation that speaks fluent memes, wields sarcasm like a lightsaber, and navigates trends like a ninja parkouring through a meme factory.

Step one: find your niche. What makes your soul vibrate? Are you the queen of slime ASMR? The undisputed champion of Minecraft parkour? The philosopher king of reaction videos? Own your corner of the internet, be the Gandalf of your chosen fandom, and build a community around your unique brand of awesome.

Next, gear up! Don't let a shaky camera or tinny audio be your downfall. Invest in decent equipment (even a tricked-out smartphone can work wonders), learn basic editing (TikTok transitions don't count!), and embrace the magic of good lighting (seriously, nobody wants to watch you film in the dark).

Now, the magic happens: content creation! Be authentic, be vulnerable, be you. Unleash your inner meme lord, drop those knowledge bombs, and tell stories that resonate. Engage with your viewers, spark conversations, and remember, laughter is the ultimate currency (well, besides actual currency, but you get the point).

And finally, the monetization fiesta! Ads, sponsorships, affiliate marketing – these are your new best friends. But don't sell your soul to the highest bidder. Partner with brands that align with your values, promote products you genuinely love, and remember, that quality content attracts the right kind of cash.

But hey, it's not all about the Benjamins. Building a YouTube empire is about connection, about creating something bigger than yourself. It's about inspiring others, sharing your passions, and maybe even leaving a dent in the universe (one hilarious cat video at a time).

According to a 2023 report by Business Insider, YouTube creators earned over $18 billion in revenue in 2022.

A 2022 study by Tubular Labs found that Gen Z spends more time watching YouTube than any other demographic.

The top 10 highest-paid YouTubers in 2023 earned over $80 million each.

YouTube Shorts, the platform's short-form video feature, is rapidly growing in popularity, offering new monetization opportunities for creators.

Remember: These are just some highlights. Be sure to do your own research and stay up-to-date on the latest trends and monetization strategies to build a successful YouTube channel.

Let's get this party started!

As Gen Z takes center stage in the digital realm, the opportunities for online entrepreneurship have never been more abundant. YouTube, with its 2 billion logged-in monthly users, provides a canvas for expression and a stage for monetization. The journey begins with the realization that your content is not just for the world to see, but also a potential source of income.

Understanding the Basics

Content is King, Queen, and Everything in Between

But here's the real magic: you're content. This is where you unleash your inner Picasso, your digital Shakespeare. Experiment with formats, find your voice and tell stories that captivate. Remember, quality over quantity; one well-crafted video is worth ten rushed uploads. Engage with your audience, respond to comments, and foster a sense of community. Your viewers aren't just numbers; they're the bricks and mortar of your YouTube kingdom. Before diving into the intricacies of monetization, it's crucial to emphasize the essence of quality content. Gen Z values authenticity, relatability, and creativity. Your content should resonate with your audience, spark conversations, and keep them coming back for more.

The Power of Niche

Identify your niche, that unique space where your passion aligns with audience interest. Whether it's gaming, lifestyle, tech, or niche hobbies, honing in on a specific audience can set you apart in the saturated world of YouTube.

Building a Community

Monetizing a YouTube channel is not just about numbers; it's about building a community. Engage with your audience through comments, social media, and live streams. A dedicated community is not only more likely to support you but also attracts potential brand partnerships.

Cracking the Monetization Code

YouTube Partner Program (YPP)

Unlocking the YouTube Partner Program is the first milestone on your monetization journey. To be eligible, your channel needs 4,000 watch hours in the last 12 months and 1,000 subscribers. Once achieved, you can earn money through ad revenue, channel memberships, and Super Chat.

Ad Revenue: The Gateway Income

Ads are the bread and butter of many YouTubers. As your channel gains traction, advertisers will pay for ad space on your videos. The more engaging your content, the higher the ad revenue.

Channel Memberships: Creating a VIP Experience

Offering channel memberships allows your subscribers to support you directly in exchange for exclusive perks like badges, emojis, and members-only content. It's a personalized way to connect with your most dedicated followers.

Super Chat: Turning Chats into Cash

Live streams are a powerful tool for engagement, and Super Chat takes it a step further. Viewers can purchase Super Chats to highlight their messages during live streams, providing a direct income stream while enhancing viewer interaction.

The Art of Collaboration and Brand Partnerships

In the world of digital entrepreneurship, collaboration is key. Building partnerships with brands that align with your content can open doors to sponsored content and affiliate marketing.

Sponsored Content: Turning Passion into Paycheck

Brands are eager to tap into your audience, and sponsored content is the bridge between creativity and commerce. From product placements to dedicated videos, collaborations can be mutually beneficial, enhancing your content while providing financial support.

Affiliate Marketing: Recommending with Rewards

Strategically integrating affiliate links into your content allows you to earn a commission for every sale generated through your referral. This not only diversifies your income but also adds value to your audience by recommending products you genuinely believe in.

Mastering the Art of Merchandise

As your brand grows, so does the demand for merchandise. From T-shirts to custom products, merchandising is a tangible way for your audience to support you while representing your brand in the physical world.

Designing Merchandise: Wear Your Brand with Pride

Collaborate with designers or unleash your creativity to design merchandise that resonates with your audience. Merch should be an extension of your brand, a wearable expression of the community you've built. All big YouTube stars make substantial amounts of money from their Merchandise business.

Dropshipping: A Hassle-Free Storefront

For those just starting, dropshipping eliminates the need for inventory management. When an order is placed, the product is directly shipped from the supplier to the customer. This allows you to focus on content creation while your merchandise business runs seamlessly in the background.

Turning Dreams into Reality

Monetizing a YouTube channel isn't just about making money; it's about turning your dreams into a sustainable reality. As a Gen Z content creator, you have the tools, the audience, and the cultural zeitgeist on your side. Seize the opportunity, embrace the digital age, and let your creativity fuel your journey to success. Remember, the greatest stories are not just told; they are lived, and your YouTube channel is the canvas upon which your narrative unfolds. The world is watching; it's time to make it worth their while.

Finding Your Tribe and Building Your YouTube Channel

Ah, the elusive niche. It's the holy grail of YouTube success, the secret sauce that separates wannabes from viral behemoths. But fear not, for this chapter is your compass, guiding you through the vast landscape of online communities and towards your tribe of devoted fans.

The Niche Whisperer: First, silence the inner critic. Your niche isn't about chasing trends or mimicking the "big dogs." It's about your passions, your expertise, and your unique spark. Think back to what makes you lose track of time, and what topics set your soul on fire. Are you the queen of DIY hacks, the master of makeup tutorials, and the comedic genius behind synchronized dog dances? Own it, embrace it, and let it be your North Star.

Deep Dive: Remember, niches aren't monoliths; they're vibrant ecosystems. Go beyond the broad strokes. Are you the "budget beauty queen" within the makeup niche? The "chill vibes" Minecraft builder? The "historical roasting" comedy king? The more specific you get, the more likely you are to attract a dedicated tribe who speaks your language and laughs at your jokes (even the bad ones).

Research is Your Friend: Don't jump in blindfolded. Dive into the YouTube trenches, and explore existing channels in your potential niche. See what resonates, what sparks inspiration, and what gaps you can fill. Analyze engagement, watch comment sections, and learn from the masters. Remember, research isn't copying; it's understanding the landscape before painting your masterpiece.

Building the Tribe: Now, let's build your palace – your channel! Craft a banner that screams your personality, write a description that's both informative and witty, and curate playlists that showcase your niche expertise. Optimize your titles and thumbnails – these are your first impressions, so make them count.

Consistency is Key: Building a loyal following takes time and dedication. Post regularly, stick to a schedule, and treat your viewers like royalty. They'll reward you with watch time, comments, and that sweet, sweet subscriber love.

Collaborate and Conquer: Remember, you're not alone in this digital jungle. Find like-minded creators in your niche, collaborate on videos, and cross-promote each other's channels. It's a win-win, expanding your reach and adding fresh perspectives to your content.

Embrace the Evolution: Trends shift, algorithms dance, and your niche might morph along the way. Don't be afraid to adapt, experiment, and explore new avenues within your core theme. Your flexibility and willingness to learn will keep your content fresh and your audience engaged.

Remember, building a successful YouTube channel isn't a sprint; it's a marathon run with epic dance parties along the way. Choose your niche with passion, craft your content with dedication, and treat your viewers like royalty. You've got the creativity, the hustle, and the internet at your fingertips. Now go forth, conquer the algorithm, and build your YouTube palace, brick by viral video, comment by comment, like by like. The internet awaits your reign!

A 2023 study by TubeBuddy found that channels with a well-defined niche see 20% higher subscriber growth than those with broader themes.

Remember: This is just a roadmap, not a rigid blueprint. Your journey will be unique, your niche will evolve, and your success will be defined by your dedication and passion. So, grab your camera, unleash your creativity, and get ready to carve your own path to YouTube stardom!

Case Study: Marques Brownlee or MKBHD

Marques Brownlee, better known as MKBHD, is a renowned technology reviewer and one of the most successful YouTubers in the tech industry. His YouTube channel has garnered over 13.5 million subscribers and 1,688,160,945 views as of January 2020[2]. So, what sets MKBHD apart from other YouTube channels?

Unique Branding

MKBHD's channel is known for its distinctive branding, which includes eye-catching thumbnails, engaging video titles, and consistent visual aesthetics. This consistent branding helps create a strong identity and makes MKBHD's content easily recognizable to his audience.

In-Depth Reviews

MKBHD is renowned for his comprehensive and detailed reviews of various tech products, including smartphones, laptops, and gadgets. His videos are informative, and entertaining, and provide valuable insights for viewers looking to make informed purchasing decisions.

Authenticity and Relatability

MKBHD's engaging and relatable personality shines through in his videos, making him a popular figure among tech enthusiasts. By sharing his personal experiences and opinions on products, he establishes a strong connection with his audience and encourages them to share their own thoughts and experiences.

Diverse Content

MKBHD's channel offers a wide range of content, including product reviews, unboxing videos, and tutorials. This diverse content strategy keeps his audience engaged and entertained, as they can find something of interest to them.

Collaborations and Sponsorships

MKBHD has collaborated with numerous brands and companies, including Google, D Brand, and other top brands. These partnerships not only provide additional revenue but also help maintain the channel's credibility and authority in the tech industry.

Consistent Upload Schedule

MKBHD posts two to three videos per week, ensuring a steady flow of content for his audience. This consistent upload schedule helps retain subscribers and attract new viewers, as they can expect fresh content regularly.

MKBHD's YouTube channel stands out due to its unique branding, in-depth reviews, authenticity, diverse content, collaborations, and consistent upload schedule. By implementing these strategies, MKBHD has built a thriving business as a successful YouTuber and a prominent figure in the tech industry.

Chapter IX

Launching Your Podcast

Bring Your Chatty Vibe Online and Build Your Brand

Forget the endless scroll of perfectly curated feeds. Forget the fleeting dopamine rush of a double tap. It's time to amplify your voice, ignite your curiosity, and build a community that goes beyond the algorithm. Gen Z, step into the world of podcasting, where the real conversations happen, the knowledge bombs explode, and the laughs crackle through your headphones like static electricity. Welcome to the dynamic world of podcasting, where the magic of storytelling meets the limitless potential of the digital age. If you're ready to make your mark in the vast landscape of online content, starting a podcast is your gateway to creativity, influence, and a thriving community. This chapter is your comprehensive guide to not just starting a podcast but building a podcast empire that resonates with your fellow Gen Zers.

Understanding the Gen Z Landscape: A Digital Renaissance

Before diving into the nuts and bolts of podcasting, let's grasp the significance of Gen Z in the digital realm. Born between the mid-1990s and early 2010s, Gen Z is characterized by its digital native status, craving for authentic connections, and an insatiable appetite for fresh, diverse content. Podcasting perfectly aligns with these characteristics, offering a platform for genuine, unfiltered conversations that resonate with the nuances of this generation. Sources: Pew Research Center, Nielsen, Edison Research

Why Podcasting? The Power of the Spoken Word

Podcasting is experiencing a renaissance and for a good reason. It's a medium that allows you to weave intricate narratives, share personal experiences, and connect with your audience in a way that text or visuals alone can't achieve. According to a study by Edison Research, 56% of Gen Z listens to podcasts regularly, making it a prime medium to captivate and engage your target audience (Source: Edison Research, The Infinite Dial 2022).

Crafting Your Unique Voice: Identifying Your Niche

In the vast ocean of podcasts, finding your niche is crucial. Consider your passions, expertise, and what makes you unique. Whether it's discussing sustainable living, reviewing the latest tech gadgets, or exploring the realms of niche pop culture, your podcast should reflect your genuine interests. This authenticity will resonate with your peers and create a loyal following.

Gen Z craves authenticity and substance. Dive into your episodes with well-researched content, intriguing storytelling, and thought-provoking discussions.

Understanding the Purpose

Before diving into the technical aspects, it's crucial to define the purpose of your podcast. Are you looking to educate, entertain, or inspire your audience? Understanding the "why" behind your podcast will shape its content, format, and overall strategy.

Key Considerations

Podcast Concept: Define a unique and compelling podcast concept that resonates with the Gen Z audience

Monetization: Explore various monetization strategies, such as sponsored advertisements and merchandise sales

Content Planning: Thoroughly plan your initial episodes, considering hosts, content, and production resources

Gear Up: Setting Up Your Podcasting Space

Creating professional-sounding content doesn't require a Hollywood studio. Invest in a quality microphone, headphones, and audio recording software. Numerous affordable options cater to budding podcasters. Once you have a clear vision for your podcast, it's time to delve into the technical aspects of setting up your show. This includes selecting the right equipment, recording, editing, and publishing your episodes. Remember, the key is delivering clear, crisp audio that keeps your audience engaged.

Equipment and Recording

Audio Quality: Invest in high-quality microphones and recording equipment to ensure professional sound quality.

Recording Environment: Create a quiet and acoustically treated space for recording to minimize background noise and distractions.

Post-Production and Publishing

Editing: Learn the basics of audio editing to enhance the overall listening experience for your audience

Hosting Platform: Choose a reliable hosting platform to publish and distribute your podcast to major streaming services

Building Your Audience

A successful podcast business hinges on building a loyal and engaged audience. Leveraging social media, community engagement, and strategic marketing will be pivotal in growing your listener base.

Audience Engagement

Engaging Your Audience: Leveraging Social Media: Your podcast's success is not limited to the audio waves; it extends to the digital realm. Leverage social media platforms like Instagram, TikTok, and Twitter to engage with your audience. Share snippets, behind-the-scenes moments, and teasers to build anticipation. In a survey by Nielsen, 73% of Gen Z reported using social media to discover new content regularly

Community Building: Foster a sense of community by encouraging listener feedback, questions, and participation in your podcast content.

Monetization Strategies

Let's be honest, even Jedi need to pay their lightsaber bills. Podcasting can be a lucrative side hustle or even a full-fledged career. Podcasts aren't just a hobby; they can be a lucrative side hustle or even a full-fledged career. Sponsorships, ad placements, premium content, and merch – the possibilities are endless. Turn your passion into profit and build a sustainable business around your voice.

Turning your podcast into a business requires strategic thinking. Explore avenues like sponsorships, affiliate marketing, and listener support. Platforms like Patreon provide a direct line for your audience to financially support your content. Remember, passion is contagious, and if your audience feels it, they'll be eager to support you.

Sponsorships: Explore potential partnerships with brands and companies that align with your podcast's values and resonate with the Gen Z demographic.

Merchandise Sales: Consider creating branded merchandise (T-shirts, Hoodies, Cap/Hat, and Mugs) that appeals to your audience and complements your podcast content.

Premium content: Offer bonus episodes, ad-free versions, or early access to new content for loyal fans who want to go deeper.

Why Podcasts? Here's the Mic Drop

Audio Alchemy: Podcasts are the ultimate multitasking magic. Learn the secrets of astrophysics while folding laundry, master the art of sourdough bread while commuting, or get your daily dose of political analysis on a walk in the park. Podcasts fit seamlessly into your already jam-packed lives, enriching your world without sacrificing a single swipe.

Beyond the Binary: Podcasts shatter the echo chambers of social media. Forget the curated algorithms feeding you the same opinions over and over. Podcasts expose you to diverse perspectives, challenge your beliefs, and spark conversations that go beyond the superficial. Prepare to have your mind blown, your heart touched, and your worldview expanded.

Community, Amplified: Podcasts aren't just solo journeys; they're vibrant communities waiting to be discovered. Join online forums buzzing with fellow listeners, attend live podcast meet-ups, or even start your own. Find your tribe, your ride-or-dies, your people who geek out over the same obscure historical fact or the latest conspiracy theory. You're not alone, and the mic is always on.

Content Creation Crown: Craving a platform to share your voice, your passion, your expertise? Podcasting is your oyster. Build your own show, interview inspiring guests, dissect the latest trends, or delve into the depths of your favorite niche. The world is your canvas, and the only limit is your imagination.

Ready to take the plunge? Here's your roadmap to podcasting glory:

Find Your Fire: What ignites your soul? What keeps you up at night, buzzing with ideas? That's your podcast topic. Niche down, go deep and own your space in the audiosphere.

Gear Up: You don't need a recording studio to get started. A decent smartphone, some basic headphones, and free editing software are all you need to launch your sonic masterpiece. As you grow, invest in better equipment, but don't let tech paralysis hold you back.

Hit Record: Script it or wing it, solo or with co-hosts, polished or raw – the beauty of podcasting is its authenticity. Embrace your unique style and let your personality shine through.

Spread the Word: Social media, online communities, podcast directories – shout your podcast from the rooftops (or at least the internet)! Create engaging snippets, trailers, and artwork. Collaborate with other creators. Let the world know your voice is worth listening to.

Connect & Thrive: Engage with your listeners, respond to comments, and answer questions. Foster a community around your show and watch it flourish. Remember, podcasting is a two-way street.

Building Your Podcast Empire

So, you've chosen your podcasting poison – that intoxicating blend of niche expertise, crackling energy, and burning desire to share your voice with the world. But where do you start? How do you transform that raw passion into a polished podcast that hooks listeners from the first "hello" and keeps them coming back for more? Buckle up, Gen Z, because this chapter is your roadmap to building a podcasting empire, brick by digital brick.

Step 1: Craft Your Sonic Oasis

Before you start, paint a vivid picture of your podcast's sonic landscape. Imagine the atmosphere you want to create. Do you want a cozy coffee shop vibe with the gentle clinking of mugs and whispered conversations? Or maybe a high-energy newsroom buzz, fueled by adrenaline and breaking headlines? Whatever your vision, translate it into tangible elements:

Music: Choose a captivating theme song that encapsulates your show's mood and sets the tone for each episode. Think upbeat jingles, introspective melodies, or even genre-bending remixes – the possibilities are endless.

Sound effects: Sprinkle in ambient sounds – the crackle of a fireplace, the gentle hum of city traffic, or the chirping of crickets – to transport listeners to the heart of your narrative.

Voice quality: Invest in a decent microphone that captures your voice's warmth, clarity, and nuances. Remember, your voice is your instrument; treat it with care!

Step 2: Master the Art of Storytelling

Podcasts aren't just audio lectures; they're journeys, adventures for the ears. Weave narratives that captivate, educate, and entertain.

Here's your storytelling toolkit:

Hook 'em quick: The first 30 seconds are crucial. Start with a bang – a thought-provoking question, a hilarious anecdote, a shocking statistic. Grab their attention and never let go.

Structure and flow: Don't let your podcast meander like a lost hiker. Create a clear structure – intro, body, outro – and navigate it seamlessly with transitions that feel natural, not forced.

Variety is the spice of life: Mix up your format. Solo rants, engaging interviews, and immersive soundscapes – keep your listeners on their toes and their boredom at bay.

Be yourself, amplified: Inject your personality into your show. Let your humor, your passion, and your quirks shine through. Authenticity is the secret sauce that makes your podcast stand out.

Step 3: Tech Titan: Taming the Tools

The world of podcasting might seem intimidating, a labyrinth of editing software, hosting platforms, and distribution channels. But fear not, young Jedi! Here's your crash course:

Editing software: Free options like Audacity or GarageBand offer surprisingly robust features for beginners. Learn to trim silences, enhance audio quality, and add music and sound effects – you'll be a sonic alchemist in no time.

Hosting platforms: Choose a reliable platform like Buzzsprout, Podbean, or Anchor to upload your episodes and distribute them to all the major podcast directories. Think of it as your podcast's home base.

Distribution channels: Apple Podcasts, Spotify, Google Podcasts – make sure your show is readily available wherever your listeners go. Remember, accessibility is key.

Step 4: Building Your Tribe: From Lone Wolf to Podcast Pack

Podcasting isn't a solo act. It's about building a community, a pack of like-minded souls who share your passion. Here's how to create your podcasting posse:

Social media: Tweet your podcast highlights, share behind-the-scenes snippets on Instagram, and spark discussions on Facebook. Remember, engagement is your friend.

Collaborations: Team up with other podcasters in your niche. Cross-promote each other's shows, co-host episodes, and tap into each other's audiences. Synergy is a powerful thing!

Live events: Organize meet-ups, host Q&A sessions, or even throw a full-blown podcast festival. Put a face to the voice and forge real-life connections with your listeners.

Chapter X

Create and Sell Online Courses & Workshops

Craving financial independence, rocking flexible hours, and sharing your fire skills with the world? Buckle up, ditch the 9-to-5 grind, and turn your knowledge into a cash machine – all from the comfort of your PJs (with killer WiFi, of course).

The digital age has transformed the way we learn, opening up new opportunities for individuals to share their knowledge and skills with a global audience. Creating and selling online courses and workshops is not only a way to monetize expertise but also to make a meaningful impact on the lives of learners worldwide. This chapter will explore the step-by-step process of establishing a successful online course business, tailored to the interests and preferences of the Gen Z demographic.

Understanding the Market

Before diving into course creation, it's essential to conduct thorough market research. Identify trending topics, niche areas of interest, and the specific needs of the Gen Z audience. Platforms like Thinkific, LearnWorlds, Skillshare and Squarespace offer valuable resources for understanding market trends and audience preferences

Why This Side Hustle Slays

Be Your Own Boss: Ditch the corporate ladder and chart your own course. You call the shots, set the pace, and build a biz that reflects your unique passions and expertise.

Location Independence: Escape the cubicle prison! Work from a beach hammock, a bustling coffee shop, or your grandma's attic – wherever your laptop and WiFi roam.

Passive Income Potential: Imagine waking up to $$ in your bank account, even while you're catching Zzz's. Create evergreen content that keeps selling while you chill or conquer new ventures.

Impact the World: Share your knowledge, empower others, and build a community around your passions. You'll be more than just a hustler; you'll be a mentor, an inspiration, and a positive force in the world.

So, you're down to slay the online course game? Here's the lowdown:

Find Your Niche and Slay It

Passion First: What sets your soul on fire? Baking sourdough bread? Building killer websites? Mastering the art of TikTok? Hone in on something you love – your enthusiasm will be contagious and fuel your content creation.

Solve Gen Z's Problems: Think like your audience. What skills do they crave? What knowledge gaps are holding them back? Focus on solving real problems and providing value that resonates with their unique needs and aspirations.

Course Creation: The course content should be engaging, interactive, and designed to deliver a high-quality learning experience. Additionally, selecting the right hosting platform is key. Options include self-hosting, online course marketplaces, and course creation software, each with its own advantages and considerations.

Craft Content that Converts

Bite-Sized Brilliance: Gen Z has short attention spans, so keep your lessons concise, engaging, and visually appealing. Think Instagram Reels meets TED Talks, with a sprinkle of humor and relatability.

Interactive FTW: Ditch the boring lectures. Gamify your courses with quizzes, polls, challenges, and live Q&A sessions. Make learning an active, rewarding experience.

Multi-format Magic: Videos, podcasts, downloadable templates, interactive exercises – cater to diverse learning styles and keep your students coming back for more.

Platform Picks

Udemy: The OG of online courses, perfect for launching your first offering and reaching a broad audience.

Skillshare: Community-focused platform ideal for creative skills like design, cooking, and music.

Teachable: Build your own branded online school with advanced marketing tools and customization options.

Kajabi: Marketing automation on autopilot? Kajabi's your jam, streamlining everything from email sequences to landing pages.

Market Like a Social Media Ninja

Insta, TikTok, YouTube – Your Stage: These platforms are where Gen Z hangs out. Create engaging content, showcase your expertise, and build a community around your course.

Collaborate and Conquer: Partner with other creators, influencers, or online communities to reach a wider audience and tap into new networks.

Offer Free Value Bombs: Share short tutorials, tips, and behind-the-scenes glimpses to attract potential students and establish yourself as an authority in your niche.

Remember, It's a Hustle

Building a successful online course business takes time, dedication, and consistent effort. But with the right passion, strategy, and a dash of social media magic, you'll be well on your way to creating a profitable side hustle that lets you be your own boss, impact the world, and maybe even buy that yacht you've been eyeing. (Okay, maybe a jet ski first, but hey, dream big!)

Get support! Join online communities, forums, and mastermind groups for course creators. Share your experiences, learn from others, and build a network of like-minded hustlers who can cheer you on and help you navigate the course creation journey.

Monetization Masters

Forget arbitrary numbers plucked from thin air. Your course price should reflect its value, your expertise, and the life-changing benefits it offers. Here's the lowdown:

Value-Based Pricing: Think about the transformation your course offers. Will it land your students their dream job? Boost their side hustle income? Help them score their perfect bae? Quantify the value and price accordingly.

Bundle Up: Offer tiered packages with bonus content, live coaching sessions, or exclusive access to your secret sauce. It incentivizes higher spending and adds perceived value.

Early Bird Specials and Flash Sales: Create a sense of urgency and exclusivity with limited-time discounts. Gen Z loves a good deal, so make them feel like they're snagging a bargain.

Subscriptions and Memberships: Keep the good vibes rolling with recurring subscriptions that offer ongoing access to fresh content, community forums, and exclusive perks. It's a win-win: consistent income for you, ongoing value for them.

Payment Playbook: Make checkout a breeze with the right payment processors. Here's your Gen Z-friendly toolkit:

Mobile-First Focus: Gen Z lives on their phones. Offer seamless mobile payment options like Apple Pay and Google Pay for frictionless transactions.

Global Currency Coverage: Expand your reach and cater to international students with currencies like Euros, Pounds, and Rupees.

Subscription Models: If you're rocking the recurring revenue game, choose platforms that handle subscriptions effortlessly.

Promotional Panache

Your course is a masterpiece, but nobody knows it exists unless you shout it from the rooftops (digitally, of course). Get creative with your marketing to stand out from the crowd.

Micro-Influencer Magic: Partner with niche micro-influencers who resonate with your target audience. Their authentic recommendations carry more weight than faceless ads.

Social Media Blitz: Unleash your inner content beast on Instagram, TikTok, and YouTube. Share valuable tips, behind-the-scenes glimpses, and student success stories.

Freebie Funnels: Offer mini-courses, downloadable templates, or webinars as lead magnets. Give a taste of your expertise and capture valuable email addresses for future marketing magic.

Community Building: Foster a thriving community around your course. Host live Q&A sessions, create online forums, and encourage student interaction. It builds loyalty and sparks word-of-mouth marketing.

Remember, monetization is not a one-time trick; it's a continuous dance. Experiment, track your results, and adapt your strategies. Analyze what works, ditch what doesn't, and keep optimizing your monetization machine.

Consider offering scholarships or payment plans to make your course accessible to a wider audience. It fosters inclusivity and attracts students who might not otherwise have the financial means.

Platform Power-Ups and Scaling Your Empire

Choosing the right platform is like picking your lightsaber – it's an extension of your power and defines your fighting style. Here's a crash course in platform kung fu:

All-in-One Warriors: Platforms like Kajabi and Podia handle everything from hosting your course to building landing pages and managing email marketing. Perfect for solopreneurs who want a one-stop shop.

Content Masters: Think Udemy and Skillshare. These platforms offer massive audiences but less customization. A great choice for launching your first course and building brand awareness.

DIY Dynamos: WordPress and Thinkific give you ultimate control over design, branding, and integrations. Ideal for tech-savvy creators who want a personalized learning experience.

Automation is Your Ally

Don't get bogged down in repetitive tasks. Embrace the power of automation to free up your time and focus on what matters – creating epic content and connecting with your students. Here's your toolkit:

Email Sequences: Set up automated email sequences to welcome new students, nurture leads, and deliver valuable content on autopilot.

Social Media Scheduling: Don't waste time manually posting. Use tools like Hootsuite and Buffer to schedule your social media content in advance.

Student Management Systems: Platforms like Teachable and LearnDash offer built-in tools for tracking student progress, managing enrollments, and sending automated feedback.

Scaling Your Course Empire

The best courses are living, breathing organisms that evolve and adapt. Here's how to take your course to the next level

Content Updates: Keep your content fresh and relevant by adding new modules, bonus materials, and live Q&A sessions.

Community Building: Foster a thriving community around your course. Host challenges, create online forums, and encourage student interaction. It builds loyalty, leads to organic marketing, and keeps students coming back for more.

Upselling and Cross-Selling: Offer bonus materials, advanced modules, or exclusive coaching sessions to high-value students. You can also create a suite of related courses and encourage students to expand their learning journey.

Partnerships and Collaborations: Team up with other course creators, influencers, or complementary businesses to reach a wider audience and expand your reach.

Remember, scaling is a marathon, not a sprint. Focus on delivering consistent value, nurturing your community, and continuously improving your course. As your audience grows, so will your profits. Don't underestimate the power of analytics. Track your student engagement, completion rates, and revenue metrics. Use this data to identify areas for improvement, personalize your content, and target your marketing efforts more effectively.

Chapter XI

Create and Sell Mobile Applications

Building Your Throne in the Gen Z Kingdom

Forget Silicon Valley suits and million-dollar boardrooms. Forget grinding away in a cubicle, dreaming of venture capital unicorns. The future of tech power lies not in corporate castles but in the pocket kingdoms of your smartphone. And who holds the keys to these kingdoms? Gen Z, the tech-savvy, socially conscious generation that scrolls with purpose and swipes with ambition.

This chapter, my friend, is your roadmap to becoming a **MOBILE APP MOGUL**, your guide to building a digital empire on the fertile ground of Gen Z's attention. Forget shoveling pixels; we're about to create interactive tapestries that will captivate, engage, and empower this influential generation.

Why Gen Z? The Golden Ticket to App Gold

Here's the truth: Gen Z is not just another demographic. They're the DIGITAL NATIVES, the ones who learned to code before they learned to tie their shoes. They crave **authenticity, personalization, and instant gratification**. They value **social causes, environmental consciousness, and mental well-being** as much as they do likes and follower counts.

78% of Gen Z spends at least three hours a day on their phones. (Statista, 2023)

They're willing to pay for premium experiences. (App Annie, 2023)

This isn't just a market; it's a goldmine waiting to be unearthed with the right app.

Unearthing Your App Idea: From Spark to Flame

But don't just chase trends, friend. Building a sustainable app empire requires a ROCK-SOLID IDEA, a diamond in the rough waiting to be polished. Look within your passions, your experiences, and your frustrations. What gap can you fill in the Gen Z landscape? What problem can you solve with a digital flourish?

Channel your activism: Build an app that connects young people to volunteer opportunities or empowers them to raise awareness about critical social issues.

Embrace the hustle: Develop a platform that helps teens manage their finances, learn new skills, or find their dream internships.

Unleash the creativity: Design an app that fosters artistic expression, encourages musical collaboration, or sparks literary flames.

Champion mental health: Create a safe space for Gen Z to talk about their struggles, access mental health resources, or build a supportive community.

The possibilities are endless. Just remember, your app should resonate with Gen Z's values, address their needs, and offer a unique experience that stands out from the crowded app store.

From Brainstorm to Build: Launching Your Mobile App Odyssey

The spark of an idea has ignited, and the call of the app store beckons. But before you dive headfirst into code and design, let's equip you with the tools and knowledge to embark on a successful mobile app journey. This chapter is your roadmap, guiding you from brainstorming to the glorious launch of your app masterpiece.

Step 1: Charting Your Course - Idea Validation and Research

Refine your concept: Is your app solving a real problem for Gen Z? Does it offer a unique value proposition? Conduct market research, talk to potential users, and validate your idea before investing time and resources.

Competitive analysis: Don't be a lone wolf. Analyze existing apps in your niche, understand their strengths and weaknesses, and identify gaps you can fill. Remember, inspiration is key, but blatant copying is a cardinal sin.

Define your Minimum Viable Product (MVP): Don't try to build the Taj Mahal of apps right away. Focus on a core set of features that deliver your core value proposition, allowing you to gather user feedback and iterate quickly.

Step 2: Building Your Dream Team - Assembling the App Avengers

Coding prowess: Do you have the programming chops to bring your app to life? If not, consider hiring freelance developers, collaborating with tech-savvy friends, or utilizing app development platforms like Thunkable or Firebase.

Design dynamo: A captivating user interface is crucial for Gen Z engagement. Find a talented designer who can translate your vision into intuitive and visually appealing screens.

Marketing maestro: Building an audience requires a marketing whiz. Partner with someone who understands social media, influencer marketing, and app store optimization to get your app noticed.

Step 3: Blueprinting Your App - Design and Development

Wireframing and prototyping: Sketch out the user flow, layout screens, and define interactions before diving into code. This ensures your app is intuitive and user-friendly.

Design iteration is your friend: Don't be afraid to test your designs with potential users and iterate based on their feedback. Remember, the app is for them, not you!

Development magic: Whether you code yourself or leverage a platform, ensure your app is secure, bug-free, and optimized for different devices and operating systems.

Step 4: Testing and Refining - Polishing Your App Gem

Beta testing is your shield: Before unleashing your app on the world, gather a group of beta testers to identify bugs, usability issues, and areas for improvement. Their feedback is gold!

Performance optimization: Speed is king in the mobile world. Test your app's performance on various devices and networks, and optimize it for a smooth and seamless experience.

App store compliance: Each app store has its own set of guidelines. Ensure your app adheres to all regulations and policies to avoid rejection and delays.

Step 5: Launch and Beyond - Taking Flight and Reaching for the Stars

Marketing blitz: The launch is just the beginning. Execute your marketing strategy, engage with your target audience, and generate buzz around your app. Social media, influencer partnerships, and app store optimization are your allies.

Analytics and feedback loop: Your app is a living, breathing entity. Monitor user behavior, gather feedback, and use it to continuously improve and iterate. Remember, your users are your compass, guiding your app's evolution.

Embrace the journey: Building a successful app is a marathon, not a sprint. Be patient, adapt to changing trends, and learn from your mistakes. The mobile landscape is dynamic, so continuous learning and improvement are key to long-term success.

Stay focused, stay passionate: The app development journey can be challenging. Remember your initial spark, your passion for solving a problem, and let it fuel your perseverance.

Celebrate the wins, and learn from the losses: Every milestone, every positive review, is a victory. And every bug, every negative feedback, is a learning opportunity. Embrace both sides of the coin.

Build a community: Connect with other app developers, share your experiences, and learn from each other. Collaboration and support are invaluable resources in the mobile world.

Conquering the App Store: Marketing Your Masterpiece

With your app polished and ready for launch, it's time to shout from the digital rooftops. But Gen Z doesn't respond to billboards and TV commercials. Here's how to capture their attention:

Social media is your warcry: Engage with Gen Z on their turf. Share sneak peeks, run contests, and build a community around your app on platforms like TikTok, Instagram, and Snapchat.

Influencer marketing is your secret weapon: Partner with Gen Z creators who resonate with your target audience to spread the word organically and authentically.

Focus on value, not just virality: Don't just chase downloads; showcase the impact and purpose of your app. Gen Z wants to know how your creation will make their lives better.

Remember, authenticity is key. Be genuine, be transparent, and show Gen Z why your app deserves a place in their digital kingdom.

Monetizing Your Mobile App: From Pixels to Profits

You've built your app, captivated Gen Z, and established yourself as a rising star in the mobile kingdom. But hey, let's be honest, even digital rulers gotta eat. This chapter, friend, is all about transforming your app into a throne of profitable pixels, a revenue engine that fuels your empire's growth.

But wait! Before you start slapping banner ads on every screen, remember this: Gen Z sees right through inauthenticity. They value experiences over blatant sales pitches. So, let's explore some monetization strategies that are as smart as they are sustainable:

1. The Freemium Model: Offer a basic version of your app for free, with enough features to hook users and showcase your value. Then, unlock premium features or advanced content through In-App Purchases (IAPs). This way, users feel they're getting something for free, while you earn from those who want the full experience.

2. Subscriptions: Think Netflix for Gen Z. For apps offering ongoing value, like educational platforms or content creation tools, a subscription model can be a goldmine. Offer different tiers with varying features and price points to cater to diverse needs and budgets.

3. Brand Partnerships: Gen Z trusts the influencers they connect with. Partner with brands that align with your app's values and target audience. Collaborate on exclusive content, limited-edition features, or sponsored experiences. This not only brings in revenue but also expands your reach and credibility.

4. Data Insights: Your app is a treasure trove of user data. Analyze user behavior, preferences, and engagement to inform future product updates, personalize the experience, and even sell insights to non-competing businesses. Just

remember, always prioritize user privacy and be transparent about your data practices.

5. Think beyond the app: Expand your empire! Create physical merchandise, organize events, or offer premium services related to your app. Diversifying your revenue streams not only boosts your bottom line, but also strengthens your brand and builds a loyal community around your creation.

Remember, monetization is not a one-size-fits-all game. Experiment, test, and iterate to find the model that resonates with your audience and fuels your app's sustainable growth.

But hold on! Running a profitable app empire isn't just about dollars and cents. It's about impact and responsibility. Use your success to give back to Gen Z. Donate a portion of your profits to causes they care about, offer scholarships or mentorship programs, or build features that promote social good. Remember, with great power comes great responsibility, and a truly noble emperor rules not just through wealth, but through positive influence.

Chapter XII

Cryptocurrency

Make Money Using Your Computer and Sixth Senses

The world of cryptocurrency has been growing rapidly, and with the rise of digital assets like Bitcoin, Ethereum, and Litecoin, investing in cryptocurrency has become an increasingly popular option for both individuals and businesses. This chapter will explore the opportunities and challenges of investing in cryptocurrency, providing valuable insights for the Gen Z demographic. We will cover various aspects of investing in cryptocurrency, including the benefits, risks, and potential business opportunities. So, let's dive in and discover the exciting world of cryptocurrency investments!

Why Invest in Cryptocurrency?

There are several reasons why investing in cryptocurrency can be an attractive option:

1. **Decentralization:** Cryptocurrencies operate on a decentralized network, which means they are not controlled by a single authority, such as a bank or government. This aspect of decentralization has made cryptocurrencies more appealing to investors who value financial autonomy and freedom.

2. **Limited supply:** Unlike traditional currencies, which are subject to inflation, cryptocurrencies have a limited supply.

For example, there is a cap of 21 million Bitcoins that can be mined, which has contributed to their value as a digital asset.

3. **Transparency:** Cryptocurrency transactions are transparent and secure, thanks to blockchain technology. This transparency can help build trust among investors and users, as it allows for easy tracking of transactions and verification of asset ownership.

4. **Lower transaction fees**: Cryptocurrency transactions typically have lower fees compared to traditional banking transactions, making them more cost-effective for businesses and individuals.

5. **Global accessibility:** Cryptocurrencies can be traded across borders, allowing investors to access new markets and diversify their portfolios.

Risks and Challenges

Despite the potential benefits, investing in cryptocurrency also comes with risks and challenges:

Market volatility: Cryptocurrency markets are known for their high volatility, which can lead to significant price fluctuations. This can make it difficult for investors to predict the long-term value of their investments.

Regulatory uncertainty: The regulatory landscape for cryptocurrencies varies across different countries and regions, which can make it challenging for businesses and investors to comply with the rules and guidelines.

Security concerns: Cryptocurrency wallets and exchanges are potential targets for hackers, and the loss of private keys can result in the loss of funds. Investors need to be vigilant about security measures to protect their investments.

Tax implications: Tax authorities in many countries are still figuring out how to treat cryptocurrency transactions, which can make it difficult for investors to understand and manage their tax obligations.

Business Opportunities in Cryptocurrency

The rise of cryptocurrency has opened up various business opportunities for entrepreneurs and investors. Some popular crypto business ideas include:

1. **Crypto mining:** This involves using computer hardware and electricity to verify transactions on a blockchain network in exchange for rewards, such as new cryptocurrency.

2. **Peer-to-peer crypto loaning:** This involves lending or borrowing cryptocurrencies through decentralized platforms, which can offer more flexible terms and lower interest rates compared to traditional financial institutions.

3. **Crypto ATM management:** Companies can provide services related to the installation and management of automated teller machines (ATMs) that accept and dispense cryptocurrencies.

4. **Opening a crypto exchange:** Entrepreneurs can establish their own cryptocurrency exchanges, which facilitate the buying and selling of digital assets.

5. **Providing consultant services:** Businesses can offer consulting services to help other companies adopt and integrate cryptocurrency into their operations.

Investing in cryptocurrency can be an exciting and lucrative opportunity for the Gen Z demographic. However, it's essential to understand the risks and challenges associated with this type of investment. By doing thorough research, setting clear investment goals, and managing risks, investors can make informed decisions and potentially benefit from the growing popularity of cryptocurrencies. As the world of cryptocurrency continues to evolve, individuals and businesses must stay informed and adapt to the changing landscape.

How to Invest in Cryptocurrency to Maximize Profitability

Investing in cryptocurrency can be a profitable venture if done correctly. This chapter will provide you with valuable insights on how to invest in cryptocurrency to maximize your returns. We will cover various strategies, risks, and best practices to help you make informed decisions.

Set clear investment goals

Before investing in cryptocurrency, it's essential to set clear investment goals. Consider the following steps:

Determine your risk tolerance: Assess your risk appetite and invest only what you can afford to lose. Cryptocurrency investments are volatile, and you should be prepared for potential losses.

Define your investment objectives: Identify your financial goals, such as capital appreciation, income generation, or diversification. This will help you choose the right cryptocurrencies and investment strategies.

Diversify your portfolio: Treat cryptocurrency as another asset class and diversify your investments across different types of cryptocurrencies and projects. This can help you manage risks and distribute your investments more effectively.

Research and select the right cryptocurrencies

Thorough research is crucial when investing in cryptocurrencies. Consider the following factors when selecting potential investments:

Market potential: Look for cryptocurrencies with a strong market presence and a history of price appreciation.

Project utility: Evaluate the practical applications and adoption potential of the cryptocurrency.

Development team: Assess the expertise and experience of the development team behind the cryptocurrency project.

Community support: Check the level of community engagement and support surrounding the cryptocurrency, as this can indicate its long-term success.

Use a reputable exchange

Choose a reliable and secure cryptocurrency exchange to ensure a smooth investment process. Research and compare different exchanges to find the best fit for your needs.

Implement a trading strategy

Develop a trading strategy that aligns with your investment goals and risk tolerance. Some common strategies include:

Day trading: Buying and selling cryptocurrencies within a short period to profit from short-term price fluctuations.

Long-term holding: Investing in cryptocurrencies with the intention of holding them for an extended period, hoping for capital appreciation.

Dollar-cost averaging: Investing a fixed amount of money at regular intervals, regardless of market conditions.

Monitor and adjust your investments

Keep a close eye on your cryptocurrency investments and be prepared to adjust your strategy as needed. Regularly review your portfolio's performance and make changes if necessary to maximize your returns.

Manage taxes and legal requirements

Be aware of the tax implications and legal requirements associated with cryptocurrency investments. Consult with a tax professional to understand the tax consequences of your investments and ensure compliance with relevant regulations.

Key metrics to consider when analyzing cryptocurrency markets

When analyzing cryptocurrency markets, there are several key metrics to consider. These metrics can help you evaluate the potential of a cryptocurrency and make informed investment decisions. Some of the most important metrics include:

Market capitalization: This is the total value of a cryptocurrency project, calculated by multiplying the current coin price by its current circulating supply.

24-hour volume: This metric represents the total value of transactions conducted within a 24-hour period, providing insight into the liquidity and trading activity of a cryptocurrency.

Supply: Understanding the total supply, circulating supply, and maximum supply of a cryptocurrency is crucial, as these statistics can greatly affect the price of a given cryptocurrency.

Price: The current price of a cryptocurrency is essential for evaluating its value and potential gowth potential.

Circulating supply: This refers to the amount of a cryptocurrency that is currently in circulation, affecting the market supply and demand dynamics.

Total supply: This is the total amount of cryptocurrency issued, including those that have been removed from circulation.

Maximum supply: This is the maximum amount of tokens that will ever be issued, which can impact the scarcity and potential value of a cryptocurrency.

Funding rates: These rates represent the cost of borrowing or lending cryptocurrencies, providing insight into market sentiment and liquidity conditions.

Open interest: This metric measures the total amount of outstanding contracts or positions held by market participants, indicating the level of market activity and interest in a particular cryptocurrency.

Stablecoin flows and exchange flows: Analyzing the movement of stablecoins and the flow of money between exchanges can provide insights into market trends and investor behavior.

Fear & Greed Index: This index monitors market sentiment by assessing market emotion and sentiment, helping investors understand the overall market atmosphere and potential opportunities or risks.

Network value to transactions (NVT) ratio*: This ratio compares market capitalization to transaction volume, providing insights into the relationship between market value and on-chain activity.

Return on Investment (ROI): This metric evaluates the performance of a cryptocurrency investment by comparing the initial amount invested across all assets.

Volatility: Measuring the price fluctuations of a cryptocurrency helps investors understand its risk profile and potential return opportunities.

Beta, Sharpe Ratio, Drawdown, and Correlation: These advanced metrics can help investors assess the risk and return characteristics of a cryptocurrency investment, providing a more comprehensive understanding of its potential performance.

By analyzing these key metrics, investors can make more informed decisions about their cryptocurrency investments and better understand the potential risks and rewards associated with each project.

Mastering Productivity

Productivity is the key to achieving your goals, both personally and professionally. In a world filled with distractions and constant demands on our time, mastering productivity is a skill that can set you apart. This chapter will guide you through various strategies and techniques to enhance your productivity, allowing you to make the most out of your time and efforts.

Set Clear Goals

The first step to being productive is to know what you want to achieve. Set clear, specific, and measurable goals for yourself. Whether they are short-term or long-term, having a roadmap will help you stay focused and motivated.

Action Steps:

- Define your short-term and long-term goals.
- Break down larger goals into smaller, more manageable tasks.
- Prioritize your goals based on their importance and deadlines.

Prioritize Tasks

Not all tasks are created equal. It's crucial to identify and prioritize your tasks to ensure that you're focusing on what truly matters. The

Eisenhower Matrix is a helpful tool for categorizing tasks based on urgency and importance.

Action Steps:

- Use the Eisenhower Matrix to categorize tasks into four quadrants: urgent and important, important but not urgent, urgent but not important, and neither urgent nor important.
- Focus on tasks in the important but not urgent quadrant to prevent last-minute rushes.

Time Management

Effectively managing your time is a cornerstone of productivity. Understand how you currently spend your time and identify areas for improvement. Techniques like the Pomodoro Technique and time blocking can be valuable in enhancing time management.

Action Steps:

- Track your time for a week to identify time-wasting activities.
- Experiment with different time management techniques to find what works best for you.
- Schedule dedicated blocks of time for specific tasks.

Eliminate Distractions

Distractions can derail your productivity. Identify common distractions in your environment and take steps to minimize or eliminate them. This may include turning off notifications, creating a dedicated workspace, or using productivity apps.

Action Steps:

- Identify your main distractions and find ways to minimize them.
- Use tools like website blockers during work periods.
- Communicate your need for focused work time to colleagues and family.

Learn to Say No

Saying no is a powerful skill in productivity. Recognize your limits and be selective about the commitments you take on. This ensures that you have the time and energy to focus on your priorities.

Action Steps:

- Assess your current commitments and obligations.
- Practice saying no politely but firmly.
- Prioritize your existing commitments and learn to decline new ones when necessary.

Continuous Learning and Improvement

Stay curious and invest in continuous learning. Explore new methods, tools, and technologies that can enhance your efficiency.

Embrace a growth mindset and see challenges as opportunities for improvement.

Action Steps:

- Allocate time for learning in your schedule.
- Attend workshops, read books, or take online courses related to your field.
- Reflect on your experiences and identify areas for personal and professional growth.

Becoming more productive is a journey that involves self-awareness, discipline, and continuous improvement. By setting clear goals, managing your time effectively, and eliminating distractions, you can build a solid foundation for productivity. Combine these strategies with a commitment to learning and saying no when necessary, and you'll be well on your way to mastering productivity and achieving your goals.